COPPERNICKEL

number 24 / spring 2017

T0155034

EDITOR/MANAGING EDITOR
Wayne Miller

EDITORS: POETRY
Brian Barker
Nicky Beer

EDITOR: FICTION & NONFICTION
Joanna Luloff

EDITOR: FICTION
Teague Bohlen

SENIOR EDITORS
Karl Chwe
Steven Dawson
Jennifer Loyd
Vin Nagle
Lyn Poats
Kyra Scrimgeour

ASSOCIATE EDITORS
Joseph Carrillo
Sammi Johnson
Taylor Kirby
Carley Tacker
Tristian Thanh

ASSISTANT EDITORS
Amber Cochran
Bri Galanaugh
Asia Groves
Carolyn Jelley
Elise Lakey
Elsa Peterson
Stephanie Rowden

INTERNS
Alison Au
Zane John

CONTRIBUTING EDITORS
Robert Archambeau
Mark Brazaitis
Geoffrey Brock
A. Papatya Bucak
Victoria Chang
Martha Collins
Robin Ekiss
Tarfia Faizullah
V. V. Ganeshananthan
Kevin Haworth
Joy Katz
David Keplinger
Jesse Lee Kercheval
Jason Koo
Thomas Legendre
Randall Mann
Adrian Matejka
Pedro Ponce
Kevin Prufer
Frederick Reiken
James Richardson
Emily Ruskovich
Eliot Khalil Wilson

ART CONSULTANTS
Maria Elena Buszek
Adam Lerner

OFFICE MANAGER
Francine Olivas-Zarate

Copper Nickel is the national literary journal housed at the University of Colorado Denver. Published in March and October, it features poetry, fiction, essays, and translation folios by established and emerging writers. We welcome submissions from all writers and currently pay $30 per printed page. Submissions are assumed to be original and unpublished. For more information, please visit **copper-nickel.org**. Subscriptions are available—and at discounted rates for students—at regonline.com/coppernickelsubscriptions. *Copper Nickel* is distributed nationally through Publishers Group West (PGW) and Media Solutions, and digitally catalogued by EBSCO. We are deeply grateful for the support of the Department of English and the College of Liberal Arts & Sciences at the University of Colorado Denver.

COPPERNICKEL

CONTENTS

FEATURE : 22 Flash Fictions

FICTION

NONFICTION

POETRY

On the Cover / Eleanor King, *Tape Loops* (detail)
colored pencil on paper, 36" x 144", 2011
courtesy of Diaz Contemporary, Toronto

(for more about King's work, visit eleanorking.com)

Editor's Note:

THE NEW YEAR, WITH ITS many changes, offers an opportunity to reaffirm *Copper Nickel*'s commitment to publishing what we consider to be the best work we receive from writers of diverse aesthetics, ethnicities, economic backgrounds, religions, nationalities, ages, sexualities, and gender identities.

While our commitment to excellence and diversity is unwavering, we're happy to say that a significant change *is* coming to *Copper Nickel* in 2017. Since our relaunch we've been laying the groundwork for paying contributors—and now, starting with issue 24, we'll be paying $30 per printed page. (We wish it could be more!)

In addition to poetry, fiction, nonfiction, and translation folios, issue 24 includes a flash fiction feature, which shows a good range of work done in the form. The *Copper Nickel* staff is grateful to fiction editors Teague Bohlen and Joanna Luloff for their sustained work in putting it together.

We're also grateful for the overwhelming response the Jake Adam York Prize has received. In our first year out of the gate we received nearly 800 manuscripts. As soon as we know the winner, we'll make an announcement via email, the *Copper Nickel* website, and social media. The winning book will be published by Milkweed Editions in the spring of 2018. And we'll begin accepting submissions for next year's Jake Adam York Prize on July 1 (due date: October 15, 2017). Next year's judge will be announced in the late spring or early summer.

As ever, thank you for supporting *Copper Nickel*, literature, and the arts. We hope you enjoy the issue.

—Wayne Miller

ALLISON CAMPBELL

New You

The new you came in a box, to your front door. You opened it and a new version of yourself inflated like a blow-up doll, pretend auto-pilot. Alligator raft. It looked good. It looked like you, but better. The parts you always suspected were not entirely part of you were missing. The parts you considered unmistakably you were exaggerated. Everything was in its better place.

But as days went the air pressure did too. The new you started looking old, like the same you you were before you got the new one. A couple days more and it looked worse—the plastic sagged heavily in areas where you had only held hair-like wrinkles.

It was work. Getting down on your knees to find the air valve, and blowing. But soon it became like brushing your teeth. It wasn't long before you became curious about how the new you had been inflated in the first place. What was its motivation, what animated it?

And you might have had time to answer this question, if you weren't so light-headed with the effort of yourself.

ADAM TAVEL

A Kindergartner's Concise History of the United States

for Al Maginnes

When they got here the fields
weren't fields. Not even green
or big flat. They had to grow
all the trees inside themselves.
The one brown road led down
to the river. George Washington
was the first one born. He rode
his horse until they made him
president. It's hard to remember
the names of any presidents
who came after. The trees
they made climb tall here
and live as woods. One tree
can't be the woods alone.
When it snows or doesn't
and all the winter cold comes
we take a piece, we take it
inside and watch it burn.

CODY ERNST

Desert Work

1.

My supervisor has a habit of marking the bodies with permanent marker,
so when we float them down the river
or elevate them with electromagnets,
we know who they are, *Howie, Jim Bob, Loretta, Gwen.*

2.

He has a definite thing for me, my supervisor.
Once, among the bodies, cataloguing, scraping,
feeding, my supervisor handed me a rose,
the type available at airport vending machines.
It was 4:30, nearly time to clock out
and go to the Korean bar in the desert;
I couldn't tell where he'd kept the rose all day.

3.

The markings my supervisor drew on the bodies
grew in their elaborateness. He abandoned names,
instead making stars, union jacks, martini glasses,
maps of the planets, bombing coordinates. Many times,
when I fueled the tanks that the bodies slept in
or culled the brownish moss that attacked the bodies' feet and hands,
I'd see him, my supervisor, off in the distance,
crouched with a fat marker, penning stuff.

4.

Most happy hours at the Korean bar continued
till morning, (we were sort of used to not sleeping
by that point) and my supervisor and I would take the Jeep out
and see how fast we could drive.
We'd race around our offices and the connected industrial facilities,
spearing flags into the ground,
pretending to be John Glenn, drunk in the lunar rover.

5.

My supervisor's marker work progressed. His designs became simpler
and more startling. Bodies began to tumble down the chute
half blacked-out
or with giant X's over their eyes. One, I remember, had a target drawn on its shaved head,
so while we spun it in the bubble-wrapper,
we were stared at alternately by a face and a bull's eye.

6.

One night a week, I stood on a podium and read to the bodies.
My supervisor, while I did this, crawled amongst them
writing words on their wrists and ankles,
Hyperbole, Discordance, Hieronymus Bosch.

7.

By the end of my supervisor's life, I'd fallen behind,
missed developments in his language.
He looked longingly at me throughout the day and night
even as his skin shriveled and his beard fell apart
and his hand began to shake too much for him to draw on the bodies
like he'd once brilliantly done. His love for me grew more profound
as I took over his duties,

testing syringes, calibrating electrodes,
balancing turntables in the ambient-music headquarters.
His affection weighed a ton.

8.

It was as though he'd completely forgotten his disappointment
the time he gave me the rose,
and I was so surprised by it
I couldn't hide my expression of horror.

T. D. STORM

Trespasses

OUR TEENAGERS, TIPTOEING AFTER DARK through the backyards and cul-de-sacs of our subdivision, spotted some strange man lurking behind garden sheds, picking the locks on detached garages. They referred to him as "The Locksmith of Oakdale Heights." At first, they said nothing to us about him for fear of implicating themselves in sneaking out after hours. But they whispered to one another, and when they needed leverage over younger siblings, who clung to them like laundered socks and nuisanced them like bees at a picnic, they scared the little ones with tales of the trespasser. If you don't leave us alone, they declared, we're going to tell the Locksmith to get you. Or, while babysitting: If you don't go to bed right now, the Locksmith will strangle you to death!

Soon, the legend invaded the little ones' playground games. Touch the wood chips, they said, and the Locksmith gobbles you up. We smiled and sniggered at one another as we listened to them make their proclamations. Kids these days; where do they get this stuff? But as one child after another fell to his or her imaginary death, we surmised that something more than youthful fancy was at play. Their shrill cries had turned shriller; their panicked scurrying across the monkey bars and rope bridge carried a sense of urgency we hadn't before seen. Who's this Locksmith? we asked as we escorted them home. And eventually they spilled the beans.

Of course, we didn't believe it. We scolded our teenagers, grounding them to their rooms on weekend nights, suspending their driving privileges. We consoled our young ones, explaining that they had nothing to worry about. But when we were together, we wondered aloud about the possibilities. Could there really be a strange man breaking into garages at night? Were we prepared for the worst case scenario—the thief, the kidnapper, the cold-blooded murderer?

Delia Pertzborn said she discovered strange footprints in the new soil she'd spread alongside her tool shed. Mark Galloway claimed someone had messed up the workbench in his three-car garage, screws and wrenches and sockets scattered everywhere. We activated our neighborhood crime watch—which is to say, we started observing more closely out our windows, beyond the reflected glare of our comfortable lives.

On the morning of June 19th, Sue Hansen saw a man exit the back door of the Forester's just before dawn. He sat on the adirondack chair on the deck and tied his shoes, then walked slowly into the woods bordering the golf course and disappeared. The Foresters were in Florida, visiting Janet's mother. Everyone knew that.

We called a neighborhood meeting. Shouldn't we contact the Forester's? someone asked. Shouldn't we call the police?

Yes, said Mark Galloway, a former police officer himself, we need a more organized response. He showed a powerpoint presentation on spotting, alerting, following through, and educating. SAFE. The police will help us, he claimed, but we also need to help ourselves. Who's with me?

We all were.

In the following days, there were several sightings of the perpetrator crossing back yards, ducking behind trash cans. Sue Hansen saw him leave the Foresters once again. His hair was wet; he was clean-shaven. Before the police arrived, Sue entered the unlocked house and examined the bathroom. Sure enough, water droplets still clung to the shower stall. A tinge of vapor edged the mirror, like the soft-focus borders of our family photos.

We bought security cameras and after multiple calls to tech support, installed them outside our homes. What we discovered disturbed us even more. Almost every night, the trespasser picked the locks of our uninhabited spaces, the overflow buildings that branched out from our homes—sheds and gazebos and occasionally a tree fort. We watched grainy black and white footage of his hooded figure as he slid his way across our yards. He crouched at doors, finagled with the knobs, and sneaked inside. Always, he'd leave before the sun rose. We never once captured his face.

How precious our children became to us then. We never let them out of our sights. We kissed them and hugged them and told them we loved them. And they—the little innocents—just wiped their faces and said, we know. When our teenagers accused us of acting all weird, we showed them the security footage and, with a degree of guilty pleasure, observed the shock and amazement that crept over their faces.

We told you, they said, and we allowed them to gloat. Don't tell the little ones, we whispered, and they complied, pleased to become co-conspirators. We urged, no, commanded them to lock the doors of their cars, to stay in groups of three at all times, to keep their social gatherings indoors. And like patriotic soldiers, they fell in line. They gathered in our basements and watched horror films on large-screen TVs. We invited our neighbors, drank wine coolers, and listened to the teens' giddy laughter float up through the air ducts underfoot. It was, oddly, a happy time.

But then our cameras caught something truly horrifying. On the morning of June 30th, the serial trespasser emerged from the basement of Doug and Audrey Johnson's house. Unlike the Foresters, the Johnsons weren't on vacation. They were home, in their master bedroom, their daughter Joni and her friend Alyssa Wilson snuggled into sleeping bags on the floor of Joni's room, watching a movie on a laptop.

It's possible the trespasser believed no one to be home; with the girls tucked away for the night, the Johnsons had gone to bed early, shutting off their lights by 10:00. Still, the thought of a stranger breaking in while we slept terrified us.

We called in locksmiths to install un-pickable dead bolts and door guards and industrial strength hasps. On the days prior to the Fourth of July weekend, the entire neighborhood was littered with vans, every locksmith in the county converging on Oakdale Heights.

Our young ones read the decals that decorated the vans in our driveways. Those too young to read overheard our slip-ups. The locksmith's coming at 11:00, we might have said. And, well, children are as vigilant as anyone, aren't they?

We assured them there was nothing to worry about, that we would always protect them and that although locksmiths did indeed exist, the predatory one their older siblings had warned them about did not. If they asked why we were changing our locks, we told them to get dressed; it was time to get out of their PJs.

Mark Galloway summoned an emergency meeting. He said we needed to form a safety patrol. He wanted people who felt comfortable with weapons. A dozen of us volunteered. We accompanied him to his garage, where he unlocked a trunk and pulled out two tasers, two paintball guns, and a billy club. He provided a brief training seminar, pointing to the various safety switches and laser sights on his artillery. If you're close enough, he said, these taser guns will take him down. They have a range of 30 feet, but you don't want to fire unless you're sure you'll hit him. If you're right next to him, you can use the drive stun feature. He removed the air cartridge and pulled the trigger, causing a blue arc to jump across the electrodes, accompanied by a rapid clicking.

The paintball guns, he explained, are filled with non-lethal pepper spray pellets. On impact, they release capsaicin, which causes irritation of the eyes and mucus membranes. We should probably know what we're getting into, he said. He fired a round of pepper at the ground, and a second later we were all coughing and covering our eyes. Our skin burned, it hurt to breathe, but we laughed and laughed anyway. We felt like daredevil kids.

Next, Mark passed around the taser and had us shock each other one by one, just so we understood the sensation of neuromuscular incapacitation. We had to do this in the academy, he said. In turn, each of us fell to the floor, screaming at the electric jolt that coursed through our bodies. The adrenaline that followed had us giggling and whooping at one another. We were ready and anxious to point our weapons at the trespasser and fire without hesitation or apology. It was going to be fun.

That night, some of us piled into Lars Larsen's minivan and drove with our lights off through the streets of our beautiful subdivision. It was a humid July evening, the air thick with moisture. A halo glowed around the moon, and bugs zig-zagged in crazy circles around porch lights. We slapped at mosquitoes and listened for crickets to cease their chirping. Near the Forester's, we exited the minivan and walked through our neighbors' backyards, tiptoeing across the grass, freezing at every twig snap and leaf rustle.

We crept around the Hansen's rose bushes and through the arbor vitae privacy hedge that edged the Doran's property. We slunk past swingsets and dipped under clotheslines; we stepped in dog doo and set off a few motion-detecting floodlights, our shadows looming. But as the night wore on and the air grew cooler, we took our time crossing the properties of our peers. We glimpsed through the shining windows a father and his teenaged son, sharing a late night snack; a couple kissing at the kitchen sink; a mother carrying a blanket-wrapped toddler off to bed—lives simultaneously our own but not our own.

We felt a sense of purpose we hadn't known for years.

On our third night, we saw someone creeping around the Pertzborn's shed. Mark hand-signalled us to split up and cover all angles of escape. We took our positions at the four corners of the yard and squinted into the darkness made darker by the various floodlights shining from the high corners of our homes.

Mark approached the shed, carrying the billy club, experienced as he was in hand-to-hand combat. The rest of us hunkered down like snipers, thumbing the safetys on our weapons, ready to ambush the violator, this thief of our security. There was electricity in the air, an encroaching summer storm rumbling through dark clouds.

Mark's flashlight danced across the exterior walls of the shed and glinted against the window panes. He tried the door, then walked the building's perimeter, shining his beam over evergreen shrubs and compost bins.

As he circled around the final corner, someone burst forth from behind a rain barrel, knocking Mark's flashlight to the ground. Freeze, Mark shouted, and we tensed like rabbits as we listened to the grunts and roars of the two struggling men thunder through the darkness. The Pertzborn's prairie grass hissed, and two shadows thrown from Mark's grounded flashlight flitted past hydrangeas and peonies. The pursuit moved like a gust of wind through the yard, over patches of weedless lawn, and through the vegetable garden, the sharp scent of tomato plants diffusing through the air. You're surrounded, Mark said.

We fingered our triggers and crouched like linemen. We flipped our tasers to drive stun mode, ready to deliver the jolt we had practiced on one another. The forest floor rustled as the chase moved off the Pertzborn's lot toward the golf course. Get him! someone screamed. We leapt from our stations. A taser rattled and a low yelp resounded through the woods.

That's what 50,000 volts feels like! Lars Larsen yelled.

But then we heard Mark say, I know! Our flashlights lit up the woods like strobes. There he goes, we shouted. There he goes.

We ran headlong, saplings lashing our faces, shouting, You can't run. Stop or we'll shoot. There's nowhere to hide.

We emerged on the seventh fairway, bent over, panting and wheezing. The moon, obscured until now, peeked out between a gap in the clouds, revealing the fleeing perp, already beyond the eighth tee, too far away to pursue.

Behind us, Mark and Lars limped from the woods.

He got away, we told them.

That's all right, Mark said. We did good tonight, boys.

We slapped each other on the back and promised to keep trying. Good work, we said. We'll get him soon.

The next night, we patrolled until 1:00 am. We shone our flashlights through every window we passed. We combed our neighbors' yards, kicking at bushes, poking in sandboxes, jumping over fences. We walked for miles that night, whispering and signaling to each other like special force commandos.

When we finally returned to Mark's garage to stash our weapons, we found the door unlocked. Mark motioned for us to ready our arms; then he kicked hard and we stormed inside. He turned on the light.

The smell of new paint permeated the air. A blaze orange message sprayed on the side wall read, You win. Mark muttered, Son of a bitch.

The paint glistened in the garage light. We touched it, and with orange-tipped fingers deduced we had just missed the trespasser.

Win what? said Lars.

But Mark shushed him. We cocked our heads and heard a scratching in the far corner, behind the boat, next to the tree-pruning equipment. Mark motioned for us to approach from both sides. We tiptoed past the pickup truck, past the lawnmower, the weedeater, past the bikes, the old baby jogger, the fridge, the workbench. We know you're in here, Mark said. Game over, scumbag.

We peered under the trailer. We unclasped the boat tarp and peeked inside. We poked at big cardboard boxes in the corner. A mouse scurried under the shelf of pesticides.

Well, we said. But there was nothing more to say.

We patrolled the neighborhood the next three nights, drove silent loops around Hope Lane and Felicity Circle. We consulted the neighbors' security footage. But the trespasser was gone. Good news, we told everyone. Life could get back to normal.

And soon, life did. We took our kids to soccer games and swim lessons, caught our teens sneaking out once more. We mowed our lawns and paid our mortgages. We argued over finances and chores. And we mostly ignored our neighbors.

But every now and then, in our quiet houses at night nowadays, we lie awake and think about the future. There will be cancers and car accidents, pregnant teens and ailing in-laws, property damage, deaths in every family. Tragedies we will be powerless to prevent.

We can't sleep. We go on solo midnight strolls through the neighborhood; cut through backyards; sometimes peer through windows at emptied, darkened houses.

We trip over basketballs and bikes left at the edges of driveways as we make our way to the park at the heart of Oakdale Heights.

It's so quiet there at night, the swing-set motionless and inert, the basketball court a silent slab of concrete. We hear crickets chirping, nothing more. We lie on the soccer field's dewy grass and stare up at the moon or the puffy dark clouds that hide it from view. And as the cool, humid air falls on our skin, we drift finally into sleep.

In the morning, when we awake, groggy from a restless night, faces puffy with worry and mosquito bites, we find we're not alone. Our neighbors—fellow insomniacs—are there beside us, yawning and itching their sticky skin. We say nothing to one another, only rise and head home, cutting through backyards and cul-de-sacs, to our children and spouses before they, too, awaken to discover us gone.

Translation Folio

LORENZO CARLUCCI

Translator's Introduction

Todd Portnowitz

LORENZO CARLUCCI WAS BORN IN 1976 in Rome, where he now teaches mathematical logic at the University of Rome "La Sapienza." His road to poetry has been a strange one—a degree in philosophy from the University of Pisa, a doctorate in mathematics from the University of Siena and another in computer science from the University of Delaware—and his poetry is appropriately strange. Part hedonist, part ascetic, his lines constantly threaten transgression. As the Italian poet Stefano Dal Bianco describes his work, Carlucci "writes with the authority of one who's understood that there's something out there to understand, and fixes on it, trudging forward, flailing, like a sort of a Thomas Aquinas dressed up as Dylan Thomas, or vice versa." All at once his voice is somehow colloquial, scientific, lyrical, severe, and comical. The form in which he most excels, with the dexterity of Charles Simic, is the prose poem—which features prominently in his two published collections, *La comunità assoluta* (Lampi di Stampa, 2008) and *Ciclo di Giuda e altre poesie* (L'Arcolaio, 2008), which together won the Premio Speciale Ceppo di Pistoia in 2009; and in his forthcoming collection, with Camera Verde press, *Sono qui solo per scriverti e non so chi tu sia.*

I first came across Carlucci's poetry in 2014, on the Italian poetry blog I co-founded and help to edit, *Formavera.* The poem was "Sono qui solo a scriverti e non so chi tu sia" ("I'm Here Only to Write You and I Don't Know Who You Are"), the title poem of the above-mentioned collection. So taken was I by the language that I translated the poem on the spot, in a sort of daze, only to return to life as usual and to my current project at the time, the translation of the poems of Pierluigi Cappello. A year later, my Cappello translations earned me a Raiziss/de Palchi Fellowship from the Academy of American Poets, with a five-week residency at the American Academy in Rome, Carlucci's native city, where I discovered his poetry a second time. At a bookstore on Via del Governo Vecchio, I picked up the latest edition of the *Quaderno di poesia contemporanea italiana* (Marcos y Marcos, 2015; *Notebook of Contemporary Italian Poetry*) edited by Franco Buffoni, a biennial anthology which has for twenty-four years brought attention to Italy's best emerging poets. Looking over its table of contents I recognized the name Carlucci, vaguely, though I wasn't sure why until I came to the page of the very same poem I'd translated the year before. By the time I'd read through the other poems of his in the *Quaderno,* and Stefano Dal Bianco's introduction to his work, I knew I had a project before me.

The sequence of poems translated below, taken from Carlucci's first collection, form a section of the book entitled "Methods." The eight "Methods" begin with a simple statement: "The thing that's still difficult, daring, is moderating your voice between song and speech." We brace ourselves for a belabored discourse on modern poetics, but what we instead get is an improvisational dialogue between the poet and his surroundings—a ticker tape of the woozy world, filtered through a frustratingly sober voice. And this is the wonder of his poetry: though the lines come off as almost mechanical, they are nonetheless insistently human, carefully recorded, deeply thoughtful. Carlucci is not merely stitching together found phrases or trying our patience with flat description, he is teasing the prose of the world into poetry.

method1

The thing that's still difficult, daring, is moderating your voice between song and speech. Spring, among its other ingenuities, has the power of gathering flowers from our lips, of stealing away our words like windblown seeds. And it does so with no concern for whether they're ripe, or confident. My sit-downs at the café, on the side of the road, in the purity of its abstract positioning, apt for receiving occasional smiles, because unforeseeable, from women and homosexuals; these sit-downs are the season's possibility. And it's the season that sharpens my gaze all at once till it reaches the end of the block, perpendicular, that makes of my eyes its vanishing point, the terminus of several shapes, three men approaching, and a fourth behind them. All of this is granted by the Spring. But it's also true that we, in turn, submit to her, as if responding to a call, to a special duty, of a clerical nature: to sit down everyday, for an agreed upon length, in a seat at the café, on the corner. And all of this so that, thanks to our observation, the street corner can hold out, can endure. Even this season's weather tires eventually, grows vulnerable. It wakes us to these mornings because it needs us, to make the world exist.

method4

Yet another, nettlesome choice, is between birdsong and Robert De Visée, during the slow, imperial fall of the pre-summer evening, when Spring reveals, in blind monologues, its true nature: the root of sleep awakening. A great sleep, to put it briefly. A sleep that begins on awakening, the happy curve of a crow above the rooftops, the revelation of a mechanism in nature. The ceiling, my dear doctors, when you stir the fireplace, expands only so it can compress, or is it the opposite? On this pre-summer evening, when it's impossible to choose, though I've already chosen, between Robert De Visée and the singing birds, between a window and a field, between a coffee and a chocolate, there appears before us, without our understanding, the face of all creation at its barest and most discreet. It's not a very pleasant face—it doesn't have, all in all, any features.

method6

For as much as you dress yourself up, you have the body of an employee. For as much as I employ myself, I have a God-like body. My hand is more beautiful than the entire street. Childhood, which is always rural, teaches us that every intention corresponds to an action, and every action to a fact, and then that fields have hearts, and grasshoppers cradles, and there's sleep in the midst of insects. And yet again, we see it clearly, that behind the problem of the famous balance between song and speech, rests the problem of our conception of the world. Whether this gentle armadillo, in its evolutions, can instill in us a gracious sense of balance. Whether we, who, if not isomorphs of ourselves, remain homomorphs of ourselves, can find daylight between the maker and the making, between a lie and a crust of earth. Because this gentle armadillo, behind us on a leash, and the problem of choosing between coming and going, or between this and that, we know, is nothing but a displacement of the central problem, of our conception of the world. As you yourself once put it, I beg you, *addresse le problème de cet homme.*

method7

A well-known problem of some importance, treated on these very shelves, is the problem of choosing, while seated at the café, whether to wait for it to get darker, and then darker. A problem disqualified by the means of its posing. We know well, my dears, with evening approaching, there will undoubtedly come that moment when it gets darker, more night-like, and that if you wait for it, you'll be confronted by the pleasant astonishment of finding yourself awaiting not the shade but the light, the point at which the day inverts. Though for every poorly stated problem there's not a solution, and he who believes to have therefore dismissed with it, is fooling himself and fooling us and this all tumbles toward a sickness. If the problem keeps posing itself, your coffee consumed, if there's still some light in the sky, if the voice of the girl speaking a foreign language, to her friend, pins you to your seat, slows your reality, close your eyes, get up and leave. Walking home you'll have night and day inside your chest, a tremendous alternating back and forth of terror and hope, but you'll also be conscious, that everything that alternates, alternates only because it's your heart.

method8

It seems, in the end, after careful analysis, that all the work of our wisdom can be reduced to a likeness with something that's hardly wise. The careful analysis of facts, which passes through an analysis of the constitution of our bodies, our pelvises, the precarious balance of grace, in the afternoon, forces us in the end to recognize that, under the sun, there's neither nothing new nor even something. The application of our wisdom, our silence, our gaze, leads us in the end to a bocce ball game with a group of retirees. In a land where the sand is white, the hands of men commanded, the thought of return a painful diversion. That all that is given to us is taken from us the same moment that it's given, cannot, any longer, arouse disquiet. And if we still fool our hearts with the idea that we have a choice between foresight and slipping from the furious watch of God, suffice it to say our wisdom is lacking.

Freedom's here under the sky, and it has no features.

Translated from the Italian by Todd Portnowitz

DAVID DODD LEE

CVS Health Corporation

The light in there is like an eclipse just before closing. The glasses I prefer have a 1980s aviator quality to them, the deliberateness of aquariums. The sharks hide in them. The primary colors are off, dulled by us, pastels everywhere else. Mayonnaise as a counterpoint to these shadings,

marbled under plastic almost, a resilient, anachronistic presence, no risk to anyone but ourselves. The dully colored antacids countenance nothing. Aspirin tablets, not for dusting with a rabbit's foot exactly, mark the proliferation of our problems. I scrawl my blood pressure

on the back of a receipt for Forever stamps. The ice cream is purple but tastes like a dim refrigerator light. I need a temptation that's larger than I know how to handle. I'm not a good shot, but the bullet moved effortlessly through the center of the Master Lock. Nonetheless, I

couldn't remove it from the shed door. A policeman drove by. *Leave me in peace,* I thought, like a sting ray, cruising down the gravel road, cardinals splashing over snow drifts & trees like blood. When I was sixteen someone pointed a muzzleloader at me. His dog panted
    smoke rings in the

late-autumn cold. Later that day we would fly in his Maverick off of Lake Harbor Road. We'd make it out alive, his car groaning into the frozen lake. Over-the-counter sleep-aids: just overpriced Benadryl. A fake fireplace on TV is not what the doctor ordered, I heard the
    pharmacist tell

a co-worker. I'd just tossed my VHS tapes into a Herby Curby. That shed was a battery hostel. It was full of weed-whackers & bug zappers ("Hang this over a cemetery stone, smelling of burned pollen & night," a friend had written on a tag hanging from one). I'm good at
    recognizing patterns

(don't even think about it!). I do not tip for barber shop quartets while I dine. $3.99 for a bottle of Yellowtail Wine! The economy is doing just fine. His headlights kept shining
    under the sheet of ice.
My new insurance information has been accepted into the system! No, ma'am, I don't
    need that in a bag.

KERRI FRENCH

The Doctor Asks Me to Describe the Pain

A kind of itch sinking beneath the water.
One eye slowly opening after surgery.
One punch to the chest. Everyone smiling.
Wax from a candle dripping to the thigh.
Happy Birthday sung through the trees as birds
taunt you in moonlight. Little coffin.
Little fingers. Green eyes squinting in the sun.
An electric cord bending back the bone.
The surgeon resting her head on your chest
and whispering *See you soon*. A kind of fever.
The body a kind of drowning. White dresses
fallen from a clothesline. A train window
slamming open, shut. Thirst of the chest.
Bird in the throat. A dog's blue growl.
The baby a kind of season. April, a kind
of stillness. Constellations shaped
like hammers. Hammers shaped like stars.

KAVEH AKBAR

Portrait of the Alcoholic with Doubt and Kingfisher

You just don't know yet which parts
        of yourself to value—
your spittle or its syrupy smell,

                your irises or their mothish obsession
        with light. Even the trap-caught fox
                knew enough to chew away its leg,

delighting (if such a thing can be said)
        at the relative softness of marrow.
Nature rewards this kind of courage—

                a kingfisher shoots into a pond
        and comes out with a stickleback.
                Starving mice will often eat their own tails

before ceding to hunger. The lesson:
        it's never too late to become
a new thing, to rip the fur

                from your face and dive
        dimplefirst into the strange.
                Some people don't even want to drink,

aren't tempted by the pools of liquor
        all around them. This seems
a selfishness. God loves the hungry

                more than the full. Faith is a story
        about people totally unlike you
                building concrete walls around their beds.

Behind each of their faces: a slowly dying
            animal. Do you feel summoned?
Do you feel heaven closing itself

                        to you like a clamshell snapping shut?
            Blessed are those who can distract themselves
                        and blessed are the distractions: a fuzzy purse

of bellyfat, a bit of mint growing wild
            along a driveway, china plates piled high with food
so pale you pepper it just to see it's there.

JOANNE DOMINIQUE DWYER

Semi-Jubilant Conversion Song

God is in the candied red syrup of the grenadine
and in the gun powder of the grenade.

He's in the ocean breeze scenting the black
hair of a woman combing the beach for colored glass—

and in the stale air in a stalled elevator shaft.

God is in the feathered head of a falcon—

       and in the hour-old embryo of a child
    conceived during a one-night stand.

Say you want a revolution—
      It's not too late to convert your way of thinking to my way of thinking.

Say you missed the Easter egg hunt the year your pelvis
     broke open like a watermelon—

and you watched the other children from your bed
       through antique opera glasses

your father bought your mother on eBay.

    Watched them scurrying around like a family of thirsty quail—

or delirious mud-caked crusaders.

All of Muhammad's sons died in infancy.
        And Fatima was his only daughter
    who did not precede him in death.

     An eclipse of the sun followed the funeral

of one of his small sons.
                    And though Muhammad

declared *The light does not darken for anyone's death*—

                        we know even savants are savaged
                by such an avalanche of loss.

Say you want to have a party for God, but you're not sure
            if he likes blood sausage—

or if he can tolerate lactose or loud hypnotic sound waves.

        It dawns on you, that you really don't know him.

Don't know what his stance is on food stamps or liposuction.

            If he prefers androgynous women—
or women who wear curlers in their hair to the supermarket.

        If he's drawn to men who carve miniature wooden animals
or men who climb poles for a living.

If he regrets creating us in a palette of colors.

And it dawns on you that you often feel
like burning yourself at the stake.

        But somehow you know that while God
                is often idle, sitting in the sun for hours
playing the pennywhistle—

        eventually he will rise up
    from the singed blue buffalo grass

        and accept our invitations
to swim across the unpolluted lake together.

JAMES DAVIS MAY

Damnation as Martin Brody

You're your own Cassandra
or worse, a minor god
in a world you wish were godless
and without intention.
A random chaotic ocean,
a collage of instinctual spasms,
dinosaur devouring dinosaur,
dumb desires causing dumber pains—that,
that you could stomach, but here,
forced to lounge on the hot sand,
looking out at the too-bright waters,
you know otherwise, you know
that the great God's looking
over your shoulder like a math teacher
delighted by your mistakes,
that your one job is to keep
that one, and that one, and that one,
and that one safe, and that
you can't. You know you'd have to touch
the water you won't touch
to know how cold it is.
So you'll watch as the boy's blood
squirts like juice from a bitten orange,
and you'll feel devastating relief
again and again to know your child is safe
not because you saved him
but because another's isn't.

JOHN McCARTHY

North End, 1997

That was the year a red & yellow Fisher Price car appeared
    on our porch, its body dented & scratched, its dirty roof
        covered in faded stickers worn down to the white adhesive.

That was the year we had plastic over the house windows
    because we had no windows. I sat on our stained porch
        in my car without windows & listened to the rain clink

the plastic roof like a clicking stove burner. That was the year
    I was always on fire because my shoes pinched my toes
        & my clothes never fit. That was the year our mailbox settled,

leaned to its side exhausted, its orange flag snapped off
    & its rusted front flap hung open like a fish's curved mouth.
        That was the year I was sent home from school for head lice,

for peeing my pants, for not changing my clothes, for never
    washing my hands. I scratched my scalp with a cheese grater
        on the porch & cried all year. That was the year I wondered

what year mom would come back. That was the year her body
    came back like a plastic toy someone had shaken with a fist.
        That was the year she slept all year. I carved my scalp open

until I could feel the smoke leaving my body. That was the year
    I stepped through a nail & my father slapped me around
        for the price of a tetanus shot. That was the year

the rest of the houses woke up covered in brown boards
    & spray paint shouting *Gas Off*. That was the year our neighbor
        was arrested for shooting squirrels with a shotgun in his yard

while I watched from a red and yellow car without moving.
    That was the year that was longer than a year in Springfield—
        gunshots—my father never speaking except to say *enough*.

S. FARRELL SMITH

Time of Death

MY MOTHER, BECAUSE IT'S NOVEMBER, is gearing up for the holiday blues. Several names on the card list are about to be scratched out. Stacks of funeral cards wait to be sorted and filed. She has a number of Catholic masses to dedicate. One cousin died suddenly from a blood clot, so she must send flowers and a donation. She clipped his obituary with vigor and relief; we bought her a small copy machine, so she can spread word of the newly deceased without having to reproduce the notices out longhand. Managing death has long been the priority, while other tasks—rearing children, cleaning out the empty nest, shoring up against deterioration, baby-proofing all over again for grand-children—have cycled.

This November day is also the end of daylight saving time, an otherwise ordinary day, both dreadful and delightful to her, as she must set the clocks back: all forty-two of them. Wall clocks, table clocks, alarm clocks. An antique mantel clock, a Waterford crystal piece, a sandstone sundial in the overgrown garden. A longcase marking the lunar phase. A terra-cotta circle on the shed. My mother is proud of her clock collection, amassed since my father's death. He was forty, my mother forty-one. Time moved on. At least to forty-two. Each hour, a wild jangling awakens the critters in the walls. Horologists would delight in my mother's midnight.

She's making her way to the family room and its four clocks when the phone rings. She jumps. My mother fears life. She worries that happiness will sneak in, and she won't be prepared to set her face in a grimace. (Worse, she'll accidentally let out a lighthearted laugh.) Nothing is life threatening, but everything in life threatens. She wears protective gear against such life. She finds the worst and weaves it into a mourning cloak wrapped tightly around her shoulders.

In the past, my mother would screen calls; now she can't make it to the phone in time. She listens to my voice filter through the wheezy answering machine. "Mom, it's me. Just wanted you to know I'm thinking of you today. I miss him too. I love you." It takes my mother a few seconds to identify which "me" has left the message. By day's end, she will have received four such communications. We daughters call when something happens. We call on holidays. And we call on each of her anniversaries: the anniversary of her father's death; of her mother's death; of her best friend's death; of her second daughter's stillbirth; of her wedding; of her husband's birth; of her husband's death, and so on. The annual sum of these messages is likely five or ten minutes.

Today, we call because it's my father's birthday. He was born nine months after the start of War Time, President Franklin Roosevelt's energy-conserving measure that moved clocks ahead and left them that way for over three years. His birthday often coincides with the end of daylight saving time. When he lived, he got one more hour to celebrate. When he died, she got one more hour to mourn.

My mother keeps moving, her thick sandy brown hair pulled into a mass atop her head and barely contained by a scarf. Shuffling across the beige kitchen linoleum, bent over her cane, she's unsteady. But she knows how to get around the house. Whenever her disease-eaten knees refuse to support her weight, my mother's knowing hands find purchase on a counter, an end table, a chair's straight back. She passes the dining-room window. Out back, beyond the brick patio that she installed where a pool used to be, stands the Memorial Garden. Spookee 1982–1995. Twinkle 1985–2000. Charcoal 1987–1996. In the graves rest brittle cat bones, wearing dolls' clothing and arranged in baskets.

On to the family room, where every square inch of wall space is adorned with an archaic farm tool, a tarnished trinket, or a musical instrument long silent. Antique glove stretchers, a broken dairy scale, the Massachusetts license plate from her parents' light-blue Ford Gran Turino, my father's orange Keds. Close to the flag that draped his coffin hangs a wedding photo in an antique brass frame. Across the top is a red ribbon, retrieved from the casket arrangement, bearing the nickname "Hon." If she plucked the picture from its tomb, she would read on the back in her own perfect cursive: *No two people loved each other more.* She would nod in agreement with herself, replace the photograph, straighten the frame, dust off the glass.

Before she was bent by her condition—a collection of some seven infections and diseases she's hiding from us and refusing to treat—my mother would drive to the town cemetery and pick leaves off the family headstone. Her own name—Dolores, from the Latin word "dolor," meaning grief or sorrow—is already etched there, next to my father's, marking the plot of earth where her body will finally rest.

After my father died, my mother asked Death to take her, too. And Death, in a manner, did. Came to her with an offer of marriage. She would live on, would provide a space for Death to flourish, with all the trappings and tokens of human life to play with, all the nooks and crannies of her house and her mind to inhabit. In return, Death would provide the income, payouts from the life insurance policy, and remain her unfailing companion until the time had come to return my mother to her husband. She accepted Death's proposal, whispering that now she would never be alone.

By the time three more messages beep on her machine, my mother makes the final turn of final clock. Forty-two hours are added, but the day is shortened.

Her own birthday most often falls on the winter solstice. Around the world each year, celebrations of the coming sunlight unfold, while my mother lies on a plastic-lined couch, and, by the glow of a heater switch and one digital clock, watches murder mysteries until she falls asleep.

BRADLEY BAZZLE

In the Presence of the Actor

JOHN PHILLIP BRAXTON HAS APPEARED in thirty-seven films and over a hundred theat-rical productions. He has played every major role in Shakespeare, from Petruchio to Prospero, and is Jean-Paul Sartre's favorite English-speaking actor. After seeing his 1956 portrayal of James Tyrone in the Broadway debut of Eugene O'Neill's *Long Day's Journey into Night*, Brooks Atkinson of *The New York Times* called Braxton "the finest actor the United States has ever produced, whose unparalleled range is now cemented."

Today, at eleven o'clock in the morning on October 20th, 1961, John Phillip Braxton is asleep in a motel room on the outskirts of Los Angeles. A thin mattress sags beneath him. Sunlight through flimsy yellow curtains gives the room a warm, candlelit quality.

The bedside phone begins to ring. The person calling is Braxton's agent, David Rosen, whom Braxton describes as a conniving flatterer. Through Rosen, Braxton has been hired for fifty-six dollars, plus expenses, to coach actors in a film called *Terror of the Haunted West*, being shot in the nearby desert.

Braxton sweeps the clamorous phone off the table and attempts, by raising the sheets over his face, to return to sleep.

The second time the phone rings, I take it upon myself to answer.

"Is this that writer?" Rosen asks.

"I'm afraid it is," I say.

"You tell Braxton they aren't paying him to sleep 'til noon. What the hell does he do all night anyway?"

I begin to describe our adventures of the previous night—a steakhouse, a cocktail bar, a karaoke lounge where Korean businessmen lavished Braxton with attention—but Rosen isn't interested. He says, "Tell Braxton that Ted locked himself in his trailer. He's gotta talk to the kid. He's the acting coach for God sakes."

Braxton whips down the sheets and sits up in bed. His eyes are puffy with sleep and his silver hair is stacked on his head. He pulls the phone from my hands and holds it awkwardly to his mouth. "Of course Ted locked himself in his trailer," Braxton says, "he read the script! One day I'll gather all the so-called writers and load them onto a Burmese slave ship."

"Then what?" Rosen asks. "You'll write all the movies yourself?"

Braxton drops the phone on the floor. He may find Rosen's comment hurtful, since he's been trying to supplement his income as an actor with that of a screenwriter. Braxton claims to have written several stirring screenplays, each with a hardboiled plot, titillating romance, and "plenty of lengthy monologues into which any actor would gladly sink his teeth." He sends these scripts to the attention of Rosen's assistant.

Braxton showers then sets about his daily ablutions: tooth brushing, hair combing, shaving followed by vegetable glycerin balm, facial exercises, vitamins, a light rinsing of the wrists and neck, five "Peter Piper's," two "Unique New York's," and all manner of creams and gelatins that I won't bother to enumerate but culminate, as always, with a ceremonious clasping of his eagle necklace behind his smooth, upright neck. The golden eagle is the only item to which Braxton seems to bear any sentimental attachment. He explains that the actor's life is a transient one, and that wearing many disguises causes "the disguises of life" to lose importance.

The phone rings again but we ignore it. Now donning a black turtleneck and crisp gray slacks, Braxton loads his tattered copy of the script into his calfskin briefcase (joking, as always, that he'll have to disinfect the briefcase when shooting is over) and we set out the door.

I accompany Braxton, who refuses to be driven, to a dilapidated diner where we enjoy a leisurely breakfast of eggs, coffee, toast, grapefruit halves, florets of broccoli, and assorted breakfast meats. There, he explains to me that the director, Roger Kitchen, is the real source of the trouble with Ted. "No doubt Kitchen has bullied poor Ted into an artless state," Braxton laments, "as the cruel sun of the American West drains life from the sand." For dessert, Braxton orders a slice of buttermilk pie.

While I pay the bill, Braxton examines a section of script. Though he tells Rosen it's such dreck he can't read it, the truth is he reads it almost constantly. He pays particular attention to the lines of Ted's character, whose words he rolls around his mouth like succulent candy.

After lunch we walk along the shoulder of a six-lane road. The sun is high and burns through the thin haze, causing the pale concrete to shimmer. Braxton, who never sweats, walks jauntily ahead while I trail behind. Sometimes he comments on buildings we pass, like a tire shop where the greasy-smocked proprietor once gave him a cup of water, or a cocktail lounge where "a real-life gaucho" asked him to dance. This starts him on a lengthy monologue about homosexuals and Montgomery Clift, whom he greatly admires. He mimics a little back and forth between Clift and Burt Lancaster in *From Here to Eternity*. "A man don't go his own way, he's nothin'!" Braxton concludes in Clift's reedy voice, then says it's a shame a young man like Clift doesn't get good work anymore.

When we crest the hill that marks the end of the ragged town, Braxton stops. He grabs my sleeve and points at the sky. "Do you see that?" he asks.

I see only haze and a few streaky clouds. "What is it?" I reply.

"Open your eyes, man. Up there! The dark spot!"

I see no dark spot, but this is not unusual; Braxton often asks if I see this or that horror, or hear a bloody scream. I never do.

"Like a filthy hair-clogged drain," Braxton whispers, "in a bathtub full of swirling clouds." He pauses for a moment while I write that down, then journeys onward.

Coming down the hill we can see the white trailers and tents to the side of the highway, where the scrubby desert stretches to the horizon in a great swath of tan. Men and women in gauzy clothes hurry between buildings, and a few skinny lights are arranged in a ring. Closer, Braxton calls my attention to two horses moored to posts behind a metal shed. "Today is horse day," he says excitedly.

As we stroll into the compound, Braxton is accosted by a small woman named Doris Jones, the line producer, whom he describes to me as "a spinster Negress."

"It's almost four," she says. "Why didn't you take a cab? We're giving you a per diem."

Braxton says he spent it on breakfast.

"We have caterers," she says, then waves to the craft-service table where burritos wrapped in tinfoil droop in the sun.

Braxton shudders haughtily. Jones grumbles about his ungratefulness then leaves. Later, Braxton will stand guard while I slide a few burritos into his briefcase.

Next comes David Rosen, who wears cowboy boots over tight slacks ("Wild Bill Shylock," Braxton calls him) and is combing his thin hair against the sandy desert wind. "Good to see you, Phil," he says. "The kid's still in his trailer. You gotta talk some sense into him."

"I *got* to do nothing," Braxton says. "I take it the young man is struggling with his poorly written character?"

"Sure."

"Good, because if he's struggling with the charlatan directing this film, then I won't be any help. In fact, I might drive Ted to suicide with my myriad tales of how much *worse* it can get in the hands of that criminal." Braxton describes a shoot in Mexico where Roger Kitchen fed the cast and crew "garbage fried in lard" for two weeks and made Braxton give line-readings to natives who later brained Kitchen with a coconut for scaring one of their donkeys into the forest with a giant rubber crab monster. Braxton retrieves the script from his briefcase and flips through it. "I have a few questions," he says. "The aliens, of what sort are they?"

Rosen sighs. "Alien aliens. Just make Ted act afraid, then heroic in the part at the end."

"You can't *act* heroic. One performs heroic acts, and that *makes* one heroic." Braxton steps away from us disdainfully and makes a loop around the craft-service table, gesticulating to himself. Rosen watches with patience. He tells me that, long ago,

Braxton decided to embrace the medium of film, in all its goofiness, and started reading science-fiction magazines with the fervor he used to reserve for Shakespeare and Ibsen.

Braxton returns to us with a calculatedly serene look and says, "Are they tall aliens with lengthy proboscises? Giant cockroach aliens with bulletproof chitinous casings? Titanian slime molds that read minds?"

"I don't know, Phil."

"Haven't they shot any of the scenes yet?"

"The aliens don't show up until the end, obviously." Rosen is referring to the common practice of saving the creature until the third and final "act" of a film, to save money on special effects and costumes. He calls out to a young woman in blue jeans, the costume girl.

"Yes, Mr. Rosen?" she says, coming towards us. She has fashionably short hair bound with a red bandana.

"What do the aliens look like?" Rosen asks.

"I'm sorry but I'm not supposed to say. Mr. Blaisdell told me to keep the aliens a secret so everybody would be scared when—"

"He wants to keep them a *secret*," Braxton says, "so it will be too late to send his lazy bones back to the drawing board."

They're referring to Paul Blaisdell, who creates all of Roger Kitchen's monsters and is famous for his budgetary mindfulness. During filming of *It Conquered the World*, when Beverly Garland threw a tantrum and destroyed the stumpy Venusian creature with a single kick to its head, Blaisdell replaced the head with a traffic cone.

"I'm sure Mr. Blaisdell knows what he's doing," the costume girl says, but Braxton has already started for the trailers. Rosen, satisfied, goes for the burritos.

I catch up to Braxton by a cluster of small trees.

"Shh!" he says. "Do you hear that?"

I listen but hear nothing.

"Hissing," he says. "It's coming from the trees, I think. Don't go in there."

I say I won't, and we continue to the trailers. There are three. Each is white and set apart from the others by a few paces. Ted's is the most dilapidated. Braxton knocks on its door.

"Go away," comes a muffled, youthful voice.

"Open up this instant," Braxton commands, and Ted does so with the alacrity of a student welcoming his master.

Ted—Theodore Gorecki—is a promising new talent Kitchen found sacking groceries in San Bernardino. He's big and handsome and has a childishly expressive round face, but today he looks wretched. He wears nothing but a robe and a baseball mitt, in which he holds a dirty tennis ball. He averts his eyes and says, "Gosh, Mr. Braxton, I just don't know about this script and—"

"We're in trouble," Braxton says. "There's a creature in the woods."

"What?"

"Let them shoot your godforsaken scene so we can get out of this place."

"It's a big scene. There'll be lots of takes."

"Tell me, Ted, how many takes were there when Gielgud played Cassius at the Royal National Theater?"

"Gosh, Mr. Braxton, I don't know."

"One, Ted. It was a play."

Ted squints.

"My point is that the excellence of your acting dictates your terms. Act well enough and you'll be on a plane tonight."

"But we still have all the scenes on the beach, the ones where the aliens capture the bikini lady to plant baby aliens inside her and I try and run 'em over in a dune buggy."

"You haven't shot those yet?"

Ted shakes his head. "And I don't know how to act it."

"Remember your training!"

"Yes, sir."

Later, Braxton will explain to me that he hated to snap at Ted but needed to get through to what he calls "the second, deeper Ted," the Ted who, "despite his torpid, childlike brain, wields a certain animal bravado for which many finer actors would sell their mothers to Arabian caliphs."

"Tell me," Braxton says, "what is my seventh rule of acting?"

Ted straightens his sloping shoulders and addresses Braxton from his diaphragm: "The power to act is the power to be any man at any time with any skill, no matter how archaic."

"Very good," says Braxton, then he leads Ted in some breathing exercises. Watching them, I wonder if it was the seventh rule that allowed Braxton, in Stratford playing the blacksmith in *Tis Pity She's a Whore*, to hammer an actual sword sharp enough to slice the little finger off a property mistress. At our first meeting, in his bachelor's apartment in the Echo Park neighborhood of Los Angeles, Braxton told me that an actor has a better understanding of how it feels to do things, to *be* things, than the man who actually does them. "A man who lived through the horrors of bubonic plague didn't spend his life preparing for those horrors," Braxton said. "He was probably illiterate. He couldn't make sense of that experience the way I can, as a trained actor."

Braxton and Ted have assumed neutral position—legs shoulder-length apart, arms at the sides, head down, eyes closed—and are taking deep breaths. This is not unusual, but there's something strange about Braxton's face, something especially intense, as if these exercises aren't for Ted's benefit but for his own. They begin whispering words into each other's faces, a technique popularized by Stanford Meisner of the Group Theatre.

Abruptly Braxton cries, "What was that!?"

"What was what?" Ted asks.

Braxton goes to the end of the trailer and presses his face to a small, dirty window. "The sky!" he says. "Why, it's the sickly sepia color of a forgotten photograph. And in the center—oh my—" He recoils from the window and presses his back against the wall of the trailer. "In the center of those swirling brown clouds a bright object was hovering. I don't know what it is, but I know it's up to no good. No good, I tell you!" With characteristic burning introspection he concludes, "What sort of hell has been unleashed on this Earth?"

"Hey," Ted says, "that's from the movie."

"Put your clothes on. We're shooting this goddamned scene. Where's Kitchen?"

Ted goes to the closet. "I can't find my costume."

"You're an actor, goddamn you. Wear a gunny sack!"

There's a knock at the door. Braxton looks through the peephole, then opens the door and pulls Rosen through it by his shirtfront.

"Take it easy," Rosen says.

"Did you see it?"

"See what?"

"The alien craft!"

"What?"

"The sky? The darkness? The swirling clouds?"

Rosen nods. "Riiiight," he says loudly, as though for Ted's benefit. "Flying saucers." He winks at Braxton and whispers, "Thanks for this, Phil."

Shockingly, at this point Braxton attempts to punch Rosen in the stomach, but Rosen spins away from him and gets behind a chair. "Okay, Phil, geez," he says.

Ted emerges wearing the gray suit and red necktie of the character he's playing, a state senator. A pair of wire glasses is perched on his broad athlete's nose. He pulls down on the suit, which is bunching in his armpits. He looks awkward and desperate.

"Here," Braxton says, then unclasps his eagle necklace and, with great solemnity, clasps it again behind Ted's thick neck. The eagle rests proudly atop the scarlet bed of Ted's necktie, and Ted squishes down his chin to regard it. I would be lying if I didn't admit that this causes in me a twinge of jealously. I've been Braxton's companion for several days and fancy we have a strong bond. I know, at least, that I'm his intellectual match in a way that Ted simply cannot be. But the bond between an actor and his master is peculiar in its strength.

"There," Braxton says, patting his trustworthy eagle, then he tells Ted a story he's never told me before: "The necklace was given to me after a particularly stirring performance of Kyd's *Spanish Tragedy*, in which I, as the Marshall Hieronimo, having gone quite mad at the conclusion of the murderous play-within-a-play, actually bit out a small piece of my own tongue and spat it onto the stage. Real blood is darker and more watery than stage blood, and it kept dribbling down my chin. This went unnoticed by all but a lovely young typist seated in the front row with her parents, who afterwards commented—very astutely, I think—that mine was an art not of man but of nature, and that watching me act was like watching an eagle rip the innards from a prone carcass. Before she left for art school in Prague, she presented me with a token of the very remark that had begun our lengthy romantic entanglement: the eagle, which daily challenges me to climb to heights of performance where only the most powerful artists dare to soar; which daily reminds me that in my core, revealed only on stage—and even then, quite tremblingly—is a majestic and bloodthirsty animal; which daily chides me to—"

Rosen interrupts the actorly reverie by opening the door and pushing Braxton through it.

A few yards from the trailer, Roger Kitchen is listening to a supporting actor named Jim Weatherby who, according to Braxton, made his name by being fat. Kitchen is tall and has the tidy look of a graduate student, which is what he was until he began making budget-minded pictures for Jim Nicholson and Sam Arkoff in 1954. Now, he is in the middle of a lucrative series based on the work of H. P. Lovecraft and starring Boris Karloff. *Terror of the Haunted West* is being shot in five days using leftover rentals from one of those films.

"I was thinking about maybe a mustache or an eye-patch," Weatherby says.

"Hmm, yes," Kitchen says, but it's plain he's only waiting for Ted and has been accosted by Weatherby, whom he indulges through tinted glasses.

Unexpectedly Braxton chimes in: "I think you're right, Jim."

"Really?" Weatherby says.

Braxton inserts himself into the narrow space between the two men, drawing the attention of several hangers on. He strokes Weatherby's cheek with the backs of two fingers and says, "A broad and noble mustache that extends past the line of your jaw and onto your neck like the wings of a swan."

Weatherby frowns.

"You heard the man," Kitchen says, and the pretty costume girl emerges from behind Kitchen and begins patting Weatherby's face with a circular sponge.

"Glad you could join us, Phil," Kitchen says. "How's the hotel? You look thin."

Braxton visibly chafes at this remark but holds his tongue. Weight is a serious subject among actors, and there is a certain type of older man who one day becomes a skeleton of himself. Braxton's luxurious meals are, in part, a bulwark against this. But Braxton only laughs and says, "I've been the same weight since first I stepped onto the stage as the star-struck Dane."

Kitchen matches Braxton's soft laugher. "And when was that?"

"Nineteen-forty or thereabouts," Braxton lies.

"Sure," Kitchen says, then tells the same story he told us yesterday, and the day before, about going with his parents to the movies and seeing an English adaptation of *A Midsummer Night's Dream* in which a young actor named John Phillip Braxton, the only American in the cast, played Lysander. "He spoke Bill Shakespeare so naturally," Kitchen says, "it was like he was sitting next to me on a train and decided to talk to me about love."

The actors and crew twitter appreciatively and cast friendly glances at Braxton, who seems genuinely embarrassed, as if the early British talkie were a youthful indiscretion. Kitchen's mouth is neutral, but from where I stand I can see behind his dark glasses, where his small eyes are wrinkled with mirth. I'm reminded of a pig's eyes.

Braxton fidgets then turns abruptly to some trees. "Ted," he says, "do you see them?"

"See who?" Ted says, then shoulders through the crowd to where Braxton is standing. Braxton pulls down on Ted's necktie until they're cheek to cheek, both men staring at the meager clump of trees.

"A forest of horrors," Braxton whispers. "You can hear them hissing. Watching us and waiting."

"Waiting for what?"

"Waiting for us to sleep so they can plant their little shrimps inside us. You know the rest. We all do, don't we? The Professor certainly does."

Ted looks confused. I should admit that I too am confused.

Kitchen touches my shoulder. "You getting this?" he whispers.

I nod curtly, disguising my confusion with diligent note-taking and the impassive expression of a journalist. The truth is I wonder if Braxton is coming unhinged, if the stress of his fringe existence in Hollywood has somehow combined with the heat and Kitchen's despotic presence to push him finally—and irrecoverably—into dementia.

Suddenly Braxton turns on us with a look of such naked terror that a few in the crowd step backwards. "They're camouflaged," he says. "Don't you see?" He walks up to Weatherby, who grabs the sleeve of the man next to him. "Can't you see them?" Braxton asks. "Can't you see their shiny black eyes between those trunks?" No one responds. Braxton looks confused. Then he backs away from us, as if *we* were the monsters. Then he runs.

Kitchen is gone from my side in an instant, hollering for the crew to follow. The entire entourage of twenty or so people shuffles towards a clearing where Braxton staggers aimlessly. I wonder why he's chosen this place until I see the skinny poles with big black boxes on top: lights. A bearded man runs up to them and fiddles with the cords. The sun has set behind a long, dusty hill, and the sky is a vivid purple peculiar to the California desert. There's a terrible crack, and Braxton is coated in white light. He runs a balletic circle around the illuminated area then stops at Paul Blaisdell, who's wiping a shiny lasergun with a rag. "Give me that," Braxton says, and Blaisdell hands it to him without ceremony. Braxton waves the lasergun over his head and marches strangely, as though entranced, towards the center of the lighted circle. Around him the shrubbery looks shiny and moonlit, like something from a richly staged opera. He gazes up at a space between two bright lights, but what does he see? I glance at the script held by Kitchen's assistant and read, "*DEAFENING WHIZ as giant silverfish-shaped SPACECRAFT weaves among treetops. CREATURES scamper beneath. SENATOR JOHNSTON braces with dignity for potential atrocities.*"

Braxton twirls to face us, furious anger contorting his face. "Get back!" he shouts. "Get back, you people! This is *my* fight!"

People glance at each other. Some leaf through their scripts.

Braxton smoothes his silver hair from his forehead, which is high and noble like that of a Civil War general, once rakish in his youth. His hands are shaking. He balls them into fists.

"Show yourselves," he says, nearly whispering. He waves the shiny gun with broad, manic movements. "You afraid of me? Fine." He throws the gun on the ground and it skitters over the flat dirt. Suddenly he gasps and takes one step backwards, and who wouldn't? For in the script I read, "*REVEAL CREATURE: tall and silver, hairless, pinheaded, with expressionless black shark-type eyes, possible wavy tendril mouth [Blaisdell? $$$?].*"

"I'm not going to hurt you," Braxton says. Then his demeanor changes. He walks forward. "No," he says. "Don't leave. We can learn so much from each other!" He runs towards the lights and falls to his knees, looking upwards so desperately that I don't even have to read along to know that the creature's "*silvery head cranes sideways, struggling to understand impassioned SENATOR JOHNSTON, and hisses before being sucked into SPACECRAFT like noodle into mouth of child. Spacecraft WHIZZES INTO SKY!!!*"

Braxton leans forward, his face in his palms, and quietly begins to weep. Someone claps, but Kitchen shushes this person. Slowly Braxton stands up, dusts his knees, and surveys the crowd. "We've got nothing to be proud of," he tells us. "Man is weak, probably the weakest creature in the universe." His gaze is stern, full of loathing for us and for himself. "Our guns haven't done anything today but scare away a superior race, one that, perhaps, would have given us a gift tantamount to fire or the wheel. I suppose we should have listened to the Professor, or at least taken the serum he developed, but now it's too late. They're gone. We're alone, and together we march towards our inevitable, private little destructions. Wasn't it Emerson who said, 'A man of genius is privileged only as far as he—'"

At this point Braxton begins a series of wild contortions and throws himself to the ground where he rolls around in the dirt. I grab the script from the assistant, flip to the last page and read, to my horror, that "*Departure only a ruse! Creature has used telepathy to IMPREGNATE SENATOR JOHNSTON with tiny shrimp-like alien fetuses!!!!!!*"

"Help me!" Braxton screams. "Help me!" Then, with disquieting understatement, he expires. For a moment I think he's really dead. I wonder if Braxton too thinks he's dead, for an instant at least. If so, he has died a thousand times. I wonder what effect this has on a person.

A single clap issues from behind me, followed by several and then a crescendo of applause and whistles and hooting.

"Well, Ted," Kitchen says above the din, "think you can do that?"

"I sure will try, Mr. Kitchen."

While Kitchen shoots take after take of Ted hollering at a man in a silver gorilla costume, Braxton gorges himself on burritos at the craft-service table. I go there to congratulate him on his performance. He seems dazed. "It isn't over," he murmurs.

David Rosen comes up and the two of them make plans to get very drunk. After that, no one approaches Braxton for a time. I wonder what people think of him: if, like me, they find his fierce commitment to fantasy somewhat troubling. Then I notice the costume girl lingering at a distance. Cautiously she slides up to Braxton and says, "I remember seeing you as a girl, with my parents."

Braxton is startled. He dabs the corners of his mouth with the back of his wrist then winks at her.

She blushes, perhaps unaccustomed to such gentlemanly trespasses. "You really are the greatest," she says.

He looks up at the sky, which is dark except for a purple streak left by the retreating sun. "Someone had to teach humanity a lesson," he says somberly, "lest the terrible events of this week lead to nothing. If only the Professor could have been here."

She nods seriously, but I can tell from her expression that she's trying to piece together his cryptic meaning. So am I. Only later will I realize that he hadn't stopped acting, or rather that he couldn't stop.

Once, early in our time together, I asked Braxton how he cried on command. It was a naïve question and one I wouldn't ask today, because it trivialized his art, but he answered that crying was simply "a matter of *experiencing* something in your head that isn't actually happening to you. It's a triumph of the mind. The only trick is if you're a person like me who doesn't cry very often. In order to cry, I must first become someone who cries and then imagine what would make *that* person cry. It's quite difficult. Sometimes—" He hesitated, as though startled by what was about to say. Then he stood up and went to the window of his apartment, which overlooked a reservoir of mysterious calm. "Sometimes I picture myself on a sort of ladder, and I can see myself, my *real* self, far below. He waves at me and I know he isn't experiencing these things. He's a happy person, I think."

When the costume girl is gone, Braxton tells me she reminds him of the girl who gave him his necklace. "A supple young creature," he says. Then he touches his chest where the eagle used to be. "Where did it go?" he asks.

I tell him he gave it to Ted. He asks me who is Ted.

"Ted Gorecki," I say and point to the circle of light where Ted is on his knees imitating Braxton's performance.

Braxton watches for a moment. "Of course," he says, "one of my finest students, with a certain animal bravado for which many finer actors would sell their mothers to Arabian caliphs. Well, what are you staring at? Write that down."

ASHLEY KEYSER

Watching Hardcore Porn in Slow-Motion

With vulpine curiosity, the camera noses its snout up to her ass
rippling extravagantly on impact. As if the act were not absurd

or tedious enough, I'm forced to linger on the dour scrotum
jowly as a venerable mayor and her buttcheeks, a fly's compound eyes.

She's got glasses, no doubt a "See me after class" prop, and a Chinese-
ish tattoo cozying up to her spine. Here the gravity-manacled body's

dream of buoyancy is granted as, mid-bounce, her breasts float
in high tan spheres, perfect as a medieval Madonna's; here his anxious,

oily pork-sword may at last stand fast without pills in troughs,
indefinitely, like a fossil. What lengths you and I, too, have gone to make

our sweaty efforts last, one-upping ourselves inside Gordian knots
made of legs. Even as our blood hurtles us to the finish, we loiter in coitus,

deferring when you'll mop your thighs in paper towels and I'll crash
into my snug little death. Better not to slow down but rewind instead:

your cum spooled up in you, us buttoned, hooked and zipped
into daytime people. If only we could stream back to that first ache,

never having touched before, your riddling body a Cyrillic letter
before I learned to pull a language from its forked silence.

Vronsky

> "A man could not be prevented from making himself a big wax doll, and kissing it. But if the man were to come with the doll and sit before a man in love, and begin caressing his doll as the lover caressed the woman he loved, it would be distasteful to the lover. Just such a distasteful sensation was what Mihailov felt at the sight of Vronsky's painting: he felt it both ludicrous and irritating, both pitiable and offensive."
>
> —*Anna Karenina*, Leo Tolstoy

Most memorable for his teeth. Not for his hunky looks
frosted in disdain, or his thighs roped around the racehorse
as her delicate spine snaps at last, but for that wall of teeth, so many
you could imagine spare rows of them, like a shark's, like ducks
at a shooting gallery. If teeth had muscles, his would bulge,
mustered against his meat in vigorous bites, clean enough
to flash back your inferior reflection. No one could compete
with that grin, but I swear I've seen his mouth before
in armies of Vronskies filing stolidly over Chemlawn pastures,
identical and upright in chinos. Vronskies slipping into infinity
pools' shallow ends: Chad and Blaine and Kevin,
torsos tapering to their hale doubles. With solo cup swigs
they down each other's loud, innocuous opinions. These men
whose cheerful banality is not the opposite of their cruelty,
but essential to it, they admire what they should love. Or they love
with the care they give their shiny mopeds, riding in twos,
the Vronsky behind resolutely not gripping his friend's hips. What
do they do to me? Why am I undone whenever one looks at me
a little too long? When we speak, is it the pleasure of his features,
so symmetrical as to be computer-generated, which loosen my
lips, limbs, burns in my throat---or just pleasure in my intelligence
as I deign, a duchess, to entertain this bronze naïf, smiling privately
at his fumbled, adorable clichés? Maybe that's why I let a Vronsky
lift me onto his kitchen counter (*so strong!*) in the nest he'd strewn
with instruments he didn't know how to play. Dangling my feet,
I watched him grapple with a sitar's neck as if he were 13 years old
and trying to get to third base. He managed at last a moan
out of that glossy belly carved in rose-garlands, the music
of a beautiful animal protesting what it must suffer.

RYAN SHARP

Bear Skins

Three brothers have draped pelts
Over their shoulders, pretending
To be bears. The first

says *Maybe father will eat too much hot porridge here*
and stay. The second

says *Maybe mother will rest her yellow head here*
and stay. The third

feels they will return to an empty house again
and stay. The first then

asks *Will our sister see our new bear suits*
and stay?

There are all sorts of violence—
the three chairs given over to heat,
the brothers' hollow wanting and what that bore
upon the previous bears.

Folding Paper

Three brothers are at the kitchen table
folding memories like paper
into birds. The first

says *I will fold the memory of us up too late watching*
Arsenio flash his immense teeth into a white loon
hovering over green water. The second

says *I will make the image of our father, handgun*
perched on the passenger seat, into a sparrow
hemmed in a bluebird box. The third feels

the story of their mother explaining AA over
dollar sundaes is too brittle to be bent
into a hummingbird. The first asks

When will our sister be back with more?

The brothers know nothing of origami, but everything
about erasure—how the moments hang prettier
from the ceiling when given feathers, wings.

The Enormous Hole

Three brothers sit in a room
with an enormous hole
in the wall. It is very cold.

The first brother says *We should do something
about the hole in the wall. It is very cold.*

Weeks later the second says *We should do something
about the enormous hole in the wall.
It has frozen our mother.*

Months pass.

The third feels the hole in the wall
is what chased away their father. The first asks

Can anyone see our sister through the hole in the wall?

After spending the better part of their twenties
observing the hole in the wall,
the brothers decide to give it a name.

J. ALLYN ROSSER

Personae Who Got Loose

Aloof, wary, notwithstanding her giddy enthusiasm for handsome misogynists and fine crystal.

So cavalier and mischievous, no one noticed that he never drank more than one glass of anything.

Anxious, extremely frugal man who lavishes every third paycheck on a charity for children in Nicaragua.

At four years she could not enjoy the ride on her carousel pony, angrily rocking and urging it forward against the pole to go faster.

He was a veteran zen buddhist with a hankering for Mounds Bars and women with multiple tattoos.

She drove a pickup and walked a muzzled Doberman, and any day of the week could fall apart completely over Greta Garbo love scenes.

Nonchalance was his middle name, in spite of his serially intense devotion to his mother's boyfriends.

The stage was full of splinters and dog hair, but people liked to lie down naked on it anyway.

CANDACE WILLIAMS

Nostrand Avenue Dirge

I am a makeshift procession crunching
down honey-leafed streets—
An acolyte to the forgotten bones whispering
under grumbling 2 trains, men
on the corner begging for smiles
and Could You Be Loved's offbeat bars rattling
car windows.
Even if solemn alchemies transform
steaming coffee to thurible
and lambswool to cossack
I cannot bear
witness for ancestors whose griots were massacred
and ink deemed criminal.
I dwell
upon their broken vertebrae and mouth
a gentle tribute.

FEATURE

22 Flash Fictions

STEPHANIE DICKINSON

Big-Headed Anna Tires of Shucking Oysters

LAFAYETTE SQUARE. 1931. No one gawks at her in The Quarter where men and women from the past roam. Men from the long ago with chocolate eyes and thin mustaches, men in Union blue uniforms, and Confederate grey men who cut their hair with butcher knives, black men with brands, dragging their manacles over cobblestone. No one asks *did you see that* when she passes. Big-Headed Anna's always the *that* except here. Mutton-chop sideburns hiding ear lobes and grizzled beards around lips about to utter red vows. The Quarter's a giant flypaper keeping pieces of what was. A one-eyed Corsican maid stealing sheets. A yellow fever brother and sister wandering the mirror thickets of Royal Street. Brown-skinned song-and-dance men painting their lips for the circuit. Mardi Gras gorging on chicory and rum, crawfish and powdered sugar beignets. No one bothers about an awkward long-legged girl, her black hair so frizzy and wild she can't keep it pinned inside her shucker's bandana. And her head *oh la la* but who cares. Big-Headed Anna's glad for the work that makes her hands weep with blood. The girl pries open the hiding places of oysters, shucking out those gobs of grit and slippery jelly, buckets of love-making food for the restaurants—Oysters Rockefeller, Oysters on the Half Shell, fried oysters. Her own childhood's been used up sitting on stones, an old broken fish knife in her fingers, her whole self crisscrossed with shell cuts. And from where Big-Headed Anna sits she sees the auction block, the naked tall black men and women like glittering charcoal, all young and strong and the smell of blood and magnolia, and sweat and vomit upon them.

JOSEPH AGUILAR

Kevin

HERE'S YOUR MILLION-dollar idea: dog mirrors.

How it works is dogface stickers on your car's wing mirrors.

As other cars approach, it appears like two dog heads thrust out joyfully.

The bus driver used to say she knew a kid who defied her by shoving his head through the open window to shout at cars.

One day a fruit truck passed too close. What remained of the kid fell back in to the floor with a noise the driver hears in dreams. Several children went to therapy for years. One boy even grew up and joined a terrorist organization.

The driver's point was to stick your head out the window is a selfish act. It could injure yourself, your peers, maybe your country.

Perhaps I'm trying to redeem something.

What I want to make up for is Kevin's death at my father's hand.

My father says it was a heart attack while returning from their walk at the beach, but when I touched the fur behind his neck, where Kevin liked to be scratched, it felt too warm, like from being in the car too long. My father must have stopped for a beer and forgotten.

Kevin's face looked sweet and open, like he knew me.

I wouldn't let my father help me bury Kevin in the ravine near the fence where I used to watch you swim laps in your parents' pool.

Did I ever tell you that?

Through the slats, near where Kevin lay, I saw you glide the water.

Another idea: Ears. Or tongues. Appendages to flap merrily in the wind.

We could use appropriate materials for the fantasy, high-grade rubber for tongues or carefully synthesized fur for ears.

I knew my father was lying.

"I was gone exactly two minutes," he said, looking up at the smoke he streamed from his mouth's corner.

"The windows were cracked open," he said, halfway into the refrigerator, searching for his rice milk.

"He was an old dog," he said, kneeling to tie his shoe.

"I'm sorry," he said, years later, finally looking in my eyes.

Also: For a higher price, maybe double, we could transform a picture of your dog's face into your sticker, though if your dog is deceased, perhaps we could offer a discount. I could see Kevin as a sticker, his ears fluttering.

It wouldn't be disrespectful. It could be celebratory.

Dogs appreciate joy, sincerity.

My favorite part about painting strangers' houses is the lift.

I like how blue the lift is, like the lowest part of the sky.

I also like when the lift lifts.

It uncurls slowly, like an arm, where I am a gift being offered.

Now I'm taping around a window. The lights in the bedroom are off. The shape of a dog lengthens over the bed, its snout out on its paws.

But the clouds part behind me, allowing light in the room. The dog is not a dog. The dog isn't even a thing. It's a collection of shadows from everything gathered around.

How I earned Kevin's respect was through my calm keel. Dogs don't like agitation. If a dog charges you, stay poised.

A dog listens to you for one of two reasons: She is afraid of you or she trusts you. The second obedience is the obedience that lasts.

Remember when I asked you to marry me?

We returned to our childhood homes, to the ravine, for the event. You brought your camera. We stayed on the path to avoid ticks.

I think we both felt pressure to perform as we should. We braced ourselves against each future we'd been threatened with.

But as I put the ring on you, it was like water settling back into itself after the swimmer goes by. We shared in the second obedience.

I have no picture of Kevin.

Phones lacked screens when I owned him.

How it worked was you took the roll of film into a store, where the clerk hid in a room to reify your memories. You got results later.

We depended less on proof of where we went or what we ate. Perhaps we believed enough to make our lives seem real. Now picures seem to generate memory.

But I think mostly why Kevin feels vivid without any proof is I was young. Experience saturates into nothing when there's too much of it.

You're right.
My million-dollar idea isn't very good.
We wouldn't do it anyway.
I'll keep painting strangers' houses.
You'll keep cutting strangers' hair.

You carried the camera into the woods for my proposal but you forgot to take a picture. Everything was overwhelmingly immediate. When we remembered, it didn't matter.
We walked toward the car holding hands.
The sky deepened over the mountains. Shadows stretched around us silently. The grass smelled sweet and open. It felt real enough to last.

ED FALCO

The Burned Boy

DAISYCUTTERS. JOSH IS the smartest, whole crew. He reads *Newsweek* every week, cover to cover. He reads books on history on culture every political screed every polemic hits the stacks in Barnes and Noble, both sides of the issue. He's fourteen, youngest in the gang, skipped a grade. Daisycutters, he explains, don't explode on impact. They shoot out an aerosol spray on the way down then detonate above ground and a square mile or more goes up in flame. People trees buildings burn or blown up by the blast or the vacuum. Two tons of explosive power. You'd be like, man, if you were there? You'd be like boom, gone! Nothin' but atoms. So we dropped these like in Iraq? Oh yeah, and Afghanistan. The press here is all Where's the Iraqi Army? Where's the Republican Guard? Dude, like, we been droppin' daisycutters on them. Where do you think they are? They're in the wind, man. They're gone.

Sometimes at night Josh dreams war. He doesn't know what he thinks. He's against the war, like his father, but he doesn't know what he thinks. His head is full of pictures: bodies falling from the windows of the Twin Towers bodies on fire Iraqi children blown to pieces a boy with arms and one leg gone white cream smeared over his torso smiling for the camera as if he's happy. Josh's dreams: the torture chambers of Saddam Hussein, mass graves, the Kurds, that eerie picture of a woman dead sprawled out dead her skin covered with a patina of white powder and in her arms her baby an infant dead, white powder. He doesn't know what he thinks but he knows what he dreams, all these pictures. In his sleep. Where the armless boy rises and floats through fire to lie beside him in his bed, still smiling. It's almost like Josh is awake. He feels like he's awake. He sees the pale blue wall in front of him in moonlight. He feels the pillow he's clutching. His back turned to the boy with no arms and no leg whose charred torso is lathered in white cream. He wants to turn and speak to the boy, but he can't. It's like his body is locked in position. When he tries to speak the words won't come. He can think the words he can almost mouth them but all that comes out are little grunting sounds little moans. He's tries to say Hello. He tries to say My name is Josh. He wants to say he's sorry for what's happened. He would like to comfort the boy if he could.

But he can't see him, the burned boy lying next to him in bed. The charred torso beside him on the sheets and Josh wants to ask him why he's smiling. But he can't speak. He doesn't have words. He wants to tell the boy that he'd help him if he could. But he can't speak. He tries in his dreams but the words won't come. He's asleep in his comfortable bed, in the suburbs of New York, the burned body of another boy silent alongside him.

Wish

CATASTROPHES. AFFLICTIONS. WISH, a freshman in high school: stage lights of the future powering up, curtain rising, and he can't find his shoes and his pants are red and he has a pimple on his nose. He has to laugh. For instance, his flat hair. It's blond and thin and strings off his head to split around ears that pop out like fleshy satellite dishes beneath his temples. Class Cut-up. Least Likely to Succeed. He's been cursed by the god of genes to look like his ugly father, an unemployed house painter, mean drunk, Aloyisus Millwright Sr., who proposes his fists will beat the screw-up into righteousness.

The day is a bully with his foot on Wish's neck. Out of his crowded trailer, through the squalid camp, along the rutted dirt road, to the crumbling asphalt that leads to the good road with the split-level houses that leads to Main Street where he walks three and a half miles to the high school preferring early rising and a long walk to being picked up by the bus at the trailer camp. Aloysius Millwright Jr. Wish. Most of his friends don't know where he lives, except Bax and Josh, because Bax has the money and Josh has the car and Wish has the connection. Together they drive over to Parrot, where the Pope lives, to score. The Pope, ex-biker turned God-fearer, believes weed is better than whiskey, likes to share a joint with the boys and talk of his days riding with the Pagans, turn each story of head-busting and whoring into a sermon which he ends with a stoned finger pointed at Wish's head as if to say Boy, are you listening?

Today Wish has a gun in his backpack. It's his father's, a Smith and Wesson .38, black, two-inch barrel. After school, he'll take the bus home with Bax, to his house with the deck that looks down over the valley, where he lives with his mother who's a professor at the college, where there are rooms full of books and magazines on the tables, where Josh and the others will meet them later, where they'll hang out in the basement and watch DVDs on the big-screen surrounded by speakers, where they'll sneak out to get high on grass Bax scored from his old babysitter; and then later, when they're all sleeping over, upstairs, in the living room, in sleeping bags on the white leather couches and wine-colored rug, he'll take it out in the darkness, in the soft light that fills up the room through long windows, he'll place it flat on the rug in that moonlight, a black jewel that will draw the boys to it. He can almost see them in his mind's eye, the boys sliding toward him as if pulled by a magnet, a black hole, dense center from which nothing escapes.

Gun in the palm of his hand in moonlight. Wish.

ROBERT LONG FOREMAN

Weird Pig

WEIRD PIG WENT to the grocery store, to look for softer mud. All he found was sand for a sandbox he didn't have. He was caught on camera, eating marshmallows in Aisle 8 straight from the bag. After a brief confrontation, he left the store snorting, vowing never to return.

Weird Pig wasn't so weird. In a lot of ways he was just like you and me. He was afraid to die, but mostly seemed to pretend it wouldn't happen to him. He didn't like the scene in *Last Tango in Paris* where Marlon Brando tells that poor woman she should have sex with the pig that throws up on people.

He remembered when the wars in Iraq and Afghanistan began, but in his heart he felt certain he would not see them end. War was a burden on the conscience of Weird Pig's generation, and it would be on his piglets' generation's conscience, too.

Oh, yes. Weird Pig was a dad.

He fell in love with Nancy Pig, who gave birth to a whole litter. Farmer Dan hollered with joy, and so did Weird Pig.

But there was one little piglet who didn't fare well. Stillborn, Farmer Dan called him. Stillborn Pig. He was one of seven pigs born that day, and the only one who didn't make it, but Weird Pig felt a part of him die when he saw Stillborn Pig's wet corpse in the straw.

They buried him behind the barn. There was no ceremony.

Weird Pig got solemn. Weird Pig drank, hiding his stash of rum behind the trough. Someone always seemed to find it, then leave it sitting out so that Weird Pig would see it there and know it had been found. They never discussed it, he and whoever it was who left it there, probably Nancy Pig. Definitely Nancy Pig.

Weird Pig was a jolly drunk, mostly, as pigs tend to be. But there was often a point in the night when for no reason Weird Pig got quiet. He got morose. He stopped making eye contact with his buddies, Jake Rooster and Bill Wyman the Mule. The laughter ran dry.

Weird Pig yelled at the piglets when he came home on the worst night he'd had in a long time. Nancy Pig pulled them close, as if to shield them from his words. He said there was no such thing as Flying Pig, which of course was true, but is not something you should dump on a piglet's head in a rage. It's cruel. Weird Pig stormed out. Nancy Pig squealed after him. He slept in the field, and when he woke up, blinking at the unforgiving sun, he heard the laughter of the Crows, Diane and Marcus Crow.

The piglets were quiet when Weird Pig stumbled in, sometime later. They didn't look at him, but Nancy Pig watched in silence as he went to the trough for some water. Nancy wished they could have their old life back. The piglets only wished he would leave.

Weird Pig saw his reflection in the trough. What he saw he hardly recognized as Weird Pig.

He turned to Nancy with tears in his eyes. He couldn't speak. He oinked with sorrow.

There was hope, though. Nancy fed him slop, talked sense into him, made him agree to drink only in moderation, no more than three nights a week.

It didn't work. A month later, after another bad night, it was clear that Weird Pig couldn't handle any drinking at all. He joined a support group at Dan's church, where at his first meeting he opened up about Stillborn Pig, and told everyone his fear of being slaughtered and eaten. They applauded him for his honesty, and he got a sponsor: Field Hand Rick.

Weird Pig stayed clean ever after. He was a model father, adored by his piglets. Nancy Pig could not have been happier.

One Christmas, Nancy Pig bought presents for each of the piglets, and Weird Pig was slaughtered so that Farmer Dan and his own offspring, Kid Bryce and Girl Pearl, could eat Weird Pig off of plates. Later, to pay for college, they went into lifetimes of debt, and Weird Pig was nothing more than the distant memory of a Christmas dinner eaten on a farm where after dinner Kid Bryce wrote a poem that went,

Thank you, Weird Pig, thank you so,
For the meat you have provided,
You've helped my arms and legs to grow
And our hunger has subsided.

It was amateur work by a well-fed but poorly educated child. It was thrown away by Farmer Dan, who thought poetry was the work of homosexuals. He forbade Kid Bryce from writing more of it.

The farm isn't there anymore. It was demolished to make way for an industrial livestock production facility, which has lots more pigs in it than the farm did. There are so many pigs, they don't even clean up all the shit that comes out of them. They just give the pigs antibiotics so they don't get infections from wading through their own waste all day.

Farmer Dan got a job working security at the grocery store. He doesn't know it yet, but he has bowel cancer, and won't live to see Kid Bryce become a man. Oh, Farmer Dan.

Janice

Everyone who is born, and everyone who dies, has one certain particular food that is more replenishing than any food or drink under the sun and sky. Better than any superfood, greater than any greatfood, it does more for the body of this certain individual than other consumables can or will.

Weird Pig's most replenishing food was pomegranate seeds. Had he eaten them every day, he would have felt better, thought more clearly, lived more happily than he ever did in his actual life, because he never ate one pomegranate seed. It's not because he didn't have a chance to eat them.

Early one morning, when Weird Pig was lying beside the stream and dozing, his friend Janice, a caterpillar, gave him a pomegranate and explained to him how to eat it. You cut it open, she said in her caterpillar whisper. You pick out the seeds.

Okay, said Weird Pig. That's exactly what I'll do. I'll wait until you leave, and then I'll cut open this pomegranate. Like you said.

Good, said Janice. She spent the next fifteen minutes walking away from Weird Pig, until she was finally out of sight.

When she was halfway gone, Weird Pig called after her, Yeah, I'm going to eat the shit out of this. All the seeds in this thing are going in my fucking mouth.

Great, whispered Janice, over her shoulder. Now she was only humoring him, where before Weird Pig had been humoring her. Mouthful of seeds, said Weird Pig, to himself, under his breath.

Janice was finally out of sight and on her way to go become a butterfly. Weird Pig went to show the pomegranate to a turtle he was friends with. He didn't know the turtle's name. The turtle knew that Weird Pig didn't know his name. He didn't care.

Check this shit out, said Weird Pig, as he wound up and threw the pomegranate at a rock wall beside which the turtle was sitting.

The pomegranate broke open and scattered seeds everywhere, like a pomegranate hand grenade.

Weird Pig couldn't stand, he was laughing so hard. When he looked over, he saw the turtle laughing, which only made him laugh more.

They laughed like that for ten minutes.

When they'd finally calmed down, the turtle explained to Weird Pig what was happening to Janice. He was telling him about metamorphosis.

Metawhatphosis? asked Weird Pig.

It's when an organism—a living organism—undergoes a change, from one original form to another form, one it was bound to become, if it lived long enough, a stage in its life cycle that was inevitable. Do you understand?

No, said Weird Pig.

No? Well, have you seen *Gremlins*?

I've seen *Gremlins 2*.

Then you're an expert already. *Gremlins 1* and *2* are—

You mean *Gremlins*.

What?

It's not *Gremlins 1*. It's just *Gremlins*.

Okay. But they're both about metamorphosis.

Okay.

In both motion pictures, the animals who terrorize people start out as mogwais.

They come out of Gizmo.

That's right, Weird Pig. In both films, they come out of Gizmo. And they end up as gremlins.

But they're not called gremlins in the movie.

Yes they are.

Are not. The working class guy in the first one *talks* about gremlins, but they never call them that.

Okay, Weird Pig. Fine.

It's true.

I thought you never watched the first one.

I thought that, too. But then when we were talking I realized I did see the first *Gremlins*.

Okay.

Not *Gremlins 1*, though. That doesn't exist.

Weird Pig went home, leaving the pomegranate seeds scattered on the ground, where some dumb birds ate them. He began printing handbills, on his laser printer, warning everyone on the farm against associating with Janice.

His handbills—which were some of his all-time best handbills—called Janice a shapeshifter, an agent of Satan. Satan was the only shapeshifter the animals and people on the farm knew about, and they had negative associations with him. Which Weird Pig was counting on. Soon they were saying that while as a caterpillar they had liked Janice and not feared her, as a butterfly she was capable of anything. Weird Pig's handbills indicated as much, but refused to offer examples of what a butterfly like Janice was capable of. The handbills left it to the reader's imagination, which was where the magic was.

Soon a perimeter was established, at the urging of Weird Pig. Torches were lit at night, and tin cans strung from wires left hanging across throughways, for fear that the new menace among them might creep in when they were sleeping.

At every opportunity—every meeting of the new Home Guard, every ice cream social—Weird Pig reminded the others how Janice had tried to poison him with a pomegranate she had laced with strychnine. He told them how she had mocked him openly, and had humiliated him many times when the others weren't around.

Janice was never seen again. Or, some said, maybe she was, because no one on the farm was entirely sure what species of butterfly Janice would have turned into. There were lots of different kinds. When they asked the butterflies they saw if they were Janice, the butterflies never said yes.

They rarely even saw butterflies, because Farmer Dan had sprayed the whole area with pesticides so lethal that most flying insects perished before coming anywhere near the barn or the house.

There was no way, they assured one another, huddled in the barn at night, that Janice could have survived the last aerial dusting they had petitioned Farmer Dan to spray across the land, with his flying drones, in the days that followed Janice's transformation. She couldn't have made it. Not with the new chemicals they used.

Janice had to be dead, long dead, her metamorphosed carcass a husk affixed forever to some high tree branch, left there in the seconds that followed the first and last flight she ever took.

Reactor

WEIRD PIG READ a book about nuclear power plants by Helen Caldicott, a pediatrician and expert on nuclear weapons, nuclear power, and the effects of radiation on human beings.

But what would radiation do to a pig like me, he wondered. What about a pig like me.

Indeed. What about me, he thought.

He really thought the word, Indeed, like that. That's the kind of pig he was.

He knew that whatever effects radiation had on pigs, it was unlikely to be as appealing as the effects radiation had on things in comic books, which is nearly always the conferral of superhuman abilities. The effects were probably more like getting cancer and/or bleeding to death from the mouth and eyes and other openings in the body, like the anus and urethra.

Weird Pig was so moved by Caldicott's book, which to be honest he read only the jacket copy of when it was handed to him by a bartender—or, not a bartender, but Freddie, who often sneaked (not snuck, Freddie insisted) behind the bar and poured drinks while the real bartender was outside, smoking—that he wrote his senator a strongly-worded letter insisting she take action on the dangers of the nuclear industry. Close the nuclear power plants, he insisted in his letter. Shut them all down before one of them melts down.

It happened that when Weird Pig's four-page email arrived at the senator's office she was, at that very moment, meeting with a lobbyist for the nuclear power industry. Their state had only one nuclear power plant, and there were plans in the works to build three more, with both private and public money, but mostly public money. Most of the power they generated would be sold to neighboring states. It will be excellent for this state's economy, said the lobbyist. *Excellent indeed*, he thought in his head—just as the senator was handed Weird Pig's email as a printout, by an aide.

Excuse me a moment, said the senator. An email has arrived from one of my valued constituents, no doubt expressing confidence in your valued industry. I'll read it aloud to you. It comes from a man called—called: Word Pig. She then read the email aloud, including the part about how the inevitable result of letting the nuclear industry gain a foothold in the region meant certain death for all living things, both in their state and across the country, because if a reactor melted down the fallout could spread halfway around the world and end life as we know it.

The more she read, the worse it got, and she kept reading it aloud, including the part about anal and urethral bleeding that made her blush, it was so graphic.

The lobbyist was baffled. He sat with his head in his hands, as the senator finished reading the letter.

How can this man—this Word Pig—know about our plans? he said. Our plans to build more reactors? It hasn't been announced at all, or anything.

The senator said, He isn't against your plans exactly, sir. He is against all such plans. All reactors, not only yours.

I am not happy, said the lobbyist. This is a terrible development. This reflects badly on you and your whole state.

He stood and prepared to leave.

I tell you what, said the senator. As proof of my and my state's dedication to your safe and clean industry I will have this man Word Pig assassinated at once. My state could stand to lose an activist who is in over his head. God knows we have enough of them.

I like what I'm hearing, said the lobbyist.

If you like that, then you'll love this. I'd like to see you douse this guy in nuclear waste and watch his flesh melt. I really would. I'd like to make sure he gets cancer from the reactors we build.

Weird Pig had forgotten all about his letter to the senator and about Helen Caldicott by the time they got around to abducting the Word Pig. The senator's security detail—loyal to a degree that sometimes frightened even the senator—had surrounded him outside his home and drugged him, so that they could bring him to a room in a hotel where the nuclear lobbyist would have 80 minutes to do with the Word Pig whatever he wanted, before they threw him off the roof of the building and made it look like a suicide.

Word Pig was not the man's real name. His real name was Brent Fialkowski, and he worked at an NPR station. It was his job to invent a different word game every week. Listeners would call in and try to solve the puzzle on the air. They would have to rearrange a bunch of letters in order to spell EIFFEL TOWER, or whatever, or take the second letter of a word the Word Pig said to them and make another word using it that was the name of a kind of food. Although the Word Pig tried to make the puzzles as easy as he could, every single caller to the station, every week, struggled to formulate correct answers to the puzzles, even the most lamebrained ones. He was embarrassed for the listener, every time. Sometimes he could be heard sighing, on the air. He thought about quitting.

They called him the Word Pig, and as impatient as he was with the callers he loved making puzzles out of words. He made them at work, for work, but he made them too as he was driving on his way to work, and as he shopped for the perfect underwear, which he could never seem to find though he tried many brands.

He made a puzzle, in his head, as he sat, kneeling, tied to the bedpost in the hotel room where the nuclear lobbyist was naked from the waist down doing lines of coke and Xanax in preparation for giving the Word Pig what he kept calling the "throat-ramming of a lifetime." He kept miming this activity, humping the air in front of the Word Pig's face, to indicate to the Word Pig what was in store for him.

He kept calling him Butterface. It's 'cause I'm gonna butt your face, he said.

The Word Pig was gagged, but he was thinking fast.

As soon as his gag was removed, by a member of the senator's security detail, he looked the nuclear lobbyist right in the eyes and said, Name the song that topped the charts in 1968 which is an anagram of *Where's my puppy's pup tent* but with two of the p's in *puppy* relocated to the letter basin, which is where you put the extra letters for the duration of this puzzle. After you complete the puzzle, the letters in the letter basin may not be repurposed in another puzzle.

The lobbyist was stunned. So were all three members of the senator's detail. Hold on a minute, he said, looking away. Just hang on. I need to write this down.

This is a lot to process, he said as he sat at the hotel room desk and began writing.

He kept writing, and saying to himself, periodically, But what's the answer?

As he worked away, furiously rearranging letters, the Word Pig strained against the bedsheet he had been tied with. The three security men stood over the lobbyist, watching what he wrote, making suggestions, attempting to solve the puzzle.

Finally, after fifteen minutes of rearranging letters—and, to their credit, not cheating by looking up the answer online—the lobbyist and the senator's guards came up with the 1968 funk hit Super! Spew up Petty Nymph, by Petty Nymph and the Star Crew. They spun around, pad of paper in the lobbyist's hand, ready to announce their triumph, but the Word Pig was gone.

He had squirmed his way out of the sheets he'd been tied with. He had made from them a rope ladder he'd used to scale the hotel's exterior wall, his throat un-rammed by the lobbyist and the senator's men, who had thought they would probably get in on that action, too, when the lobbyist was done.

The answer the lobbyist had come up with, while a great try, was not in fact the correct answer. He had forgotten to use the letter basin—had forgotten that two of the p's from the word *puppy* were to go in the letter basin so that the puzzle can be properly solved.

The correct answer was Unpretty, Humpy Sweeps—as in, the lesser-known 1968 rock and roll hit Humpy Sweeps by the band Unpretty, who had made a modest name for themselves opening for Fairport Convention, before their only successful record-ing, Humpy Sweeps, put them on the map momentarily, just before their untimely breakup.

The lobbyist never knew his answer was wrong. And he never let on to the sen-ator that the Word Pig had gotten away. He let her assume that the throat-ramming had gone off without a hitch and that the Word Pig, opponent to her nuclear plans, was dead. He wasn't, but no one cared, and the senator never learned otherwise. She didn't listen to NPR. They built the three reactors without substantial opposition from anyone in the state or out of it.

RUTH JOFFRE

In Tidy Print

THERE WAS A letter, yes. A brief unsigned missive with the words I love you written in tidy print on a sheet of slate gray cardstock. It was discovered late on the morning of the 15th when an officer investigating reports of an abandoned vehicle down by Clear Creek stopped at the address listed on the registration (an apartment on E. Davenport). There was gold lettering on the front of the house to indicate that there were actually two apartments, one above, one below, but he didn't have an exact number, and without it he went with the one that was quiet; that was how he found the letter: on a table on the porch. He wouldn't have noticed it, except it had been sealed in a dark red envelope and rather than send it through the regular mail the writer had taped it to the lid of a large white pastry box—it didn't even have an address or stamp on it. When no one answered the door, he decided to investigate the box further. Inside it was an assortment of homemade desserts alongside a card listing the contents: bourbon vanilla caramels, cranberry almond shortbread, and a tiny strawberry shortcake decorated with rose petals. That meant she'd been gone for two days.

His colleagues asked him how he knew. It was in the placement of the letter: whoever left it knew her curtains would be open on Valentine's Day, was familiar enough with her apartment's layout to know her desk was right next to the window, and picked a spot on the porch table rather than leaving it at her doorstep because they'd wanted her to see it first thing Friday morning. This was the kind of gift you were proud of, worried about; they would've spent weeks planning it and the better part of a day assembling the ingredients, arranging everything just so; how heartbroken they must've been when she didn't call; how disappointing to see the box still sitting there so long after. He imagined they were worried—sending texts, asking if she was okay. In the back of their mind they would've been wondering, is she seeing someone else? Has she been with them all this time? He'd considered the possibility, but dismissed it as unlikely. He'd assumed kidnapping ever since patrols in Tiffin communicated the circumstances of the car's discovery: the trunk open and the snow the night before; the farmhand who'd reported it said it looked like the driver slid on the ice and left to find help, but uniforms confirmed there hadn't been anyone heading toward the gas station when they passed it and no one remembered seeing anything suspicious; they had found a set of footprints, though: men's size fourteens—that was what worried him.

None of her friends were real suspects. He spoke to as many of them as he could that first day and didn't find anything. Most of them were in the dark about her private life, said she'd been an actress in New York before moving to Iowa and because of this they felt like they never really got to know her. No one thought she had a boyfriend but many suspected she had a girlfriend she was keeping hidden (she did that sometimes; they never understood why). Her upstairs neighbors hadn't seen anyone and had only met her once, but did say that she was pretty—thin frame, green eyes; when it got cold she wore a full-length jacket, but in the spring you could see her figure. He thought maybe there was something to their attraction, but they'd been out of town and had the receipts to prove it; and her other neighbors didn't know her at all. This was up near the university in an area populated by grad students—no one knew anyone. If that pastry box had been there much longer, it would've been stolen. He was surprised raccoons hadn't gotten to it; based on what he'd learned in the interviews, it must've been left sometime between midnight Thursday and 8AM on Friday, when the neighbors first remembered seeing it. Her friend had come over Thursday evening for a drink and didn't think it was there when she left around eleven—and no, she wasn't the one. They had fooled around once before but were just friends then. In fact, her friend said she seemed very happy with her secret lover; she'd never seen her so nervous, so shy: she didn't want to screw this up. Thursday before Valentine's Day, she went shopping at the Co-Op and seemed to be planning something special; the receipt listed pomegranate, mascarpone, and honey, raw honey. There was a recipe for crepes in her search history, but then—nothing. That was the night she was taken.

He assumed that there were two men: the one with size fourteen feet, and the one with the snow chains who'd driven them in the storm. He'd noticed while heading back to the precinct that her apartment was just two blocks up from a late-night convenience store, just three blocks away from a popular bar, and off a major thoroughfare, and if not for the timing he'd probably say it was a crime of opportunity; but to take someone on Valentine's Day you'd have to mean it, he thought. These weren't just lonely drunks walking home from the bar and thinking hey this woman saying goodbye to her friend is real pretty, maybe we should take her. It occurred to him that they might've known her, in passing, might've seen her in the street or in the classroom. Her occupation was listed as student, teaching assistant—were these undergraduates, then? He didn't like to think of the disgruntled athletes and linebackers in her rhetoric class taking their frustrations out on her, and he spent the better part of a day running down her students and checking all their alibis (they all checked out). He even made inquiries at the university, but she didn't have any enemies they knew of, and her work was great; they'd been happy with her. It must've felt like life was getting so good. Nice job, new love. He'd eaten one of the caramels and knew whoever made them loved her very much. He didn't consider them a suspect.

There was some concern expressed for the baker's heart. An officer at the precinct, seeing the gift with its red red letter and cold candied petals, said, "Oof, that's rough," and then sat down and refused to speak of it again, keeping his thoughts to himself even after they'd found the body, wrapped in twine and dumped in a snow bank down by Clear Creek. There seemed no point in it, then: the cake, which had been so lovingly prepared and which, in the cold snap after Valentine's Day, had frozen stiff and smooth until it was almost too pretty to eat (though it was eaten, quietly and in sections, the same day he brought it in, while the officers and detectives stood around with their long faces). In between bites, they were able to determine a few things: that this baker was a female, most likely, age twenty to thirty-five, with a well-developed palate and a refined sense of presentation; that she would have in her possession a number of specialty baking tools, including but not limited to: a candy thermometer, a star-shaped cookie cutter, a spring-form ring mold (for the cake), and a stainless steel icing spatula for spreading frosting; that her handwriting was neat, when it needed to be, though the hands themselves were small and thin and her heart was broken, as theirs were in pure sympathy. Then someone pointed out that sometimes when the evidence of love disappears the love itself ceases to exist, and so they finished the cake (they destroyed every last trace of it), and then went on with their lives in the hopes that one day the baker's love would die and her heart would be free to love again.

DANIELLE LAZARIN

Back Talk

WHEN THE BOY who barely speaks says to you, *it's too bad, who you are*, into your ear at a party, you know better than to turn your head. You know who he is. It's when he whispers, *too bad, who you belong to*—this word: belong—that your body responds, a shiver he can't detect but that makes you step back towards him. *Because damn*, he says then, *what I wouldn't do to you*. Next he says it dirty, in detail, so quietly no one else knows it's happening. Is it? Do you, after listening, still as a statue while he leans into your ear from behind but doesn't touch you, yet—go with him to a stairway outside the party, slipping out that side door in the kitchen, knowing you'll have to come back for your jacket later, alone? The boy you are dating is his friend. Not his best friend. He is dating a freshman on your track team, but you don't hang out with her. Her first boyfriend. Her first heartbreak.

You don't answer him. You don't even look at him but he knows to leave his beer behind on the counter, to sit down on the steps a flight up from where the party continues, everyone you know in that packed, parent-free apartment, neither one of you remembering to care. Has it happened? Have you unzipped his pants, plunged your hand in before you've even kissed, your name falling from his mouth like a plea, a spell? In your memory, the stairwell is bright, too bright. And your hand, your mouth around him, a reward for him even speaking to you, for saying what you didn't know you wanted to hear. Your boyfriend doesn't talk either. He doesn't talk about your body or your friends or his friends or his family who you have seen from a distance of fifty feet but never met, the family he is away with right now. Has it happened, you kneeling on the landing, his zipper against your chin, his head thrown back in surprise, how goddamned loud he is all of a sudden, the shock of what he asked for, how much more he received. When you stop, he asks for a tissue.

Has it happened? Of course it has. The boy who does not speak has told everyone by Tuesday. You, though, choose to stay silent: to your boyfriend, to that asshole, to his girlfriend, who believes him, because it's easy to believe what you hear when there is no back talk.

Now, your boyfriend is talking: Was it worth it? Did you like it? Did you think you could get away with it? And you, too, have questions: Was it worth it? Did you like it? Did you think you could get away with it? The questions are for the asshole, the one who, by the time you graduate fifteen months later, single, you realize you've never said a word to. In the stairwell, you just shook your head.

PATRICIA COLLEEN MURPHY

Tattoo

It was the size of a Franc that I traced on lined paper. Green, as if the name my father gave me was not Irish enough. The design in the middle was a scrawl born from the letters T R I S H—the name I gave myself, the name of my rebirth, the clean-break name. I had fallen in love, and the tattoo was her idea.

She was a wisp. Tall but 20 pounds lighter than me. I could not keep my eyes off her sail of red hair. She taught me to smoke, to put my finger down my throat and vomit in the parking lot so that I could accept more free drinks from the line of men I had never known existed because I was so busy asserting myself.

We lived together for a year—first in Luxembourg, with a host family provided by the college, then in a two-room apartment in France that we rented ourselves—walking to the electric company and telephone company and water company to turn everything on. We pulled the fold-out mattress out of the couch and put it in the corner where we slept together most nights, unless one of us had found someone to go home with. We studied at cafés. Both of us burning through men as quickly as cigarettes and rough bottles marked in block letters, Vin Rouge.

One day she borrowed my skirt. Halfway to the bus stop she looked down and screamed "I'm naked!" We could see her coat, but not the floral fabric of the piece I lent her. We retraced our steps, thinking it had fallen. Then I lifted her coat. It had ridden up around her tiny waist.

Hers was on her shoulder, also a design with the letters of her name. Later she would cover it with a daisy. It wasn't because we grew apart, which we did, or that we changed our names, which we didn't. It was because we had them inked at a tiny parlor in a German town we can't remember the name of, and though we weren't drunk, the artist was, and our designs ended up looking like piles of tangled ants.

My plastic surgeon is appealing in ways I never considered to be an option. Teeth in tight white rows, pore-free smooth skin, full brown hair in luscious curls, and Spanish eyes. I think he would like to sleep with me. Even if he might want to fix me a little first. Some Botox for the forehead, lift the breasts so they face his eyes instead of his knees. I wonder what might happen if I asked him? Not to sleep with me, but if he ever thought about it. I just want to know.

He hands me some safety glasses then puts on his own pair. We smile at each other with goggle-dy faces. My ankle is laid bare upon the table. My eighth treatment. He knows how much this hurts me so he always asks me a question first, he listens closely, then starts the laser when I don't expect it. He's really good with the wand—I know because my first treatment was with someone who took ten minutes to burn the edge of the circle. He takes ten seconds. If he needs to go in again, he looks sheepish. Distracts me. Green, it turns out, is the hardest of the colors. A stubborn spot that won't come out.

THOMAS LEGENDRE

John McEnroe's Omelet

WHY WOULD KELLY recognize him at table six? He orders a tomato and spinach omelet with hash browns. This is SoHo. This is the 1990's. You only see what you expect to see. True, there's something familiar about him. The smooth bars across his forehead, the high hairline, the set of his eyes. But at first Kelly is caught by his companion, a redhead in a short skirt, legs bladed like scissors, swinging her gaze through other people as if afraid of seeing them. Kelly knows that look from the inside-out. It's the look of a woman who can't quite square her circles with men, trying to appeal and conceal at once.

When Kelly stops by their table to ask how's everything, she freezes at the sight of his empty plate. That's when she puzzles out his face. Wrinkles deeper. Hair graying and cropped closely. No headband, no tennis whites, no pout. But you don't need vintage video to call it a match.

Through the kitchen hatch Juan tells her McEnroe owns a gallery nearby. An art gallery? Come on. You can't be serious, man. You cannot be serious.

He becomes a regular, two or three times a week along with the other dealers and artists, the low-altitude execs, the untagged wildlife. The omelet disappears every time. Does he chew? He's pleasant and polite. He tips twenty-five percent. It's a welcome break from the ladies bussed in from the retirement home on Long Island every Tuesday morning who all want decaf with their meal, not before, so it's fresh and hot, the B&T gagglers asking what flavor coffees do you serve? Coffee-flavored coffee. Don't even ask about the food. There's enough heat in her day to keep her warm at night. McEnroe is an easy serve and return, with his girlfriend on some kind of tropical starvation diet.

Until one day she isn't there. McEnroe sits alone with his empty plate, reading the *Times* and staring out the window. Kelly knows that look too. While she's refilling his coffee he spots the infinity symbol on her wrist.

"A tattoo," he says, "is a permanent record of a temporary attitude."

She leans upright with the coffee pot, hand on hip. "Like video of someone yelling at an umpire."

"Regrets. I've had a few."

"But then again," she says, "infinity washes it all away. It goes on forever, with or without us. That's the point."

He gestures vaguely at the air. "We used to think the ocean was infinite. We used to think the stars were fixed. And now what? We don't even know if it's a single universe any more. Is it a multiverse? Is it expanding forever? Or will it contract and crush us in the end?"

"This is what happens when you read the Science section."

He smiles sadly. "And the Sports."

Should she show him her other wrist? A circle with a diagonal line. The empty set. Everything on one hand, nothing on the other. It could have been a real slash, blade against skin, to mark her unfinished math degree, her boyfriend's wandering eye, but that was a momentary wish.

She nods at his empty plate. "How's the omelet?"

"Is or was?"

"Answer my question." She says it softly. "The question, jerk."

His eyes brighten for a vivid instant like a ball hitting the line, chalk flying up. "Good and gone."

WENDY OLESON

When a Child Dies (Bear It Away)

IT ISN'T EASY to bury a boy with fish-colored eyes.

Can you see?

Take off your hat (it covers your eyes) Put on your hat (it shades the sun) Wrap him in silk (Ask about the father) Drink moonshine on the water (Please don't ask about the father) Mom left the boy (Didn't drown him) The lake did it (Dad didn't help) Nobody's to blame the (we're all) fish (slippery, cold). Our tails flicker in the grass like nostrils against a baby's scalp. Flicker inside yourself (and) see with one fish eye.

None of this could have been helped.

PEDRO PONCE

Mel Brooks

THE SPANISH MEL Brooks was waiting for a train. I watched as he scanned the arrivals and departures overhead. He mumbled slowly to himself, maybe the name of a destination or a platform number. The Spanish Mel Brooks bore an uncanny resemblance to the American Mel Brooks. But the Spaniard seemed more serious. The Spanish Mel Brooks would probably never lead a song and dance about the Spanish Inquisition.

I have a theory that in a past life, I was in the Spanish Inquisition, the non-musical version. I don't think I was a member of the clergy, at least nothing requiring complicated vestments or one of those heavy hats. I was probably pretty smart for my age, too literate for manual labor, though also too sensitive to work a torture machine. I was, most likely, a scribe who recorded official proceedings. American me has lost centuries of digital dexterity on keyboards and screens. But Spanish me was probably pretty fast with a quill and inkpot. I also probably took my job very seriously. Obsessed with getting down every last detail, I would have invented my own system of inquisitorial shorthand. I could not simply draw in the margins of my parchment, say, a wave to signify death by drowning or flames to signify burning at the stake. I've never been good at drawing, and between my disappointment in myself for being such a bad drawer and my confusion as I attempted to decipher just what punishment was being designated by the clumsy abstractions emerging from my pen, I would miss valuable information. Underline *valuable*. Underline *information*. Exclamation point!

I suspect if I were the reincarnation of a sub-inquisitor, I was sent back in order to use my powers of transcription for good instead of evil. This would explain why I'm so good at hindsight and data entry, but not so good at foresight and spectator sports.

It would be good to introduce myself, I thought as the schedule board purged its tiles of the last hour. When I looked again, the Spanish Mel Brooks was gone. He must have had a train to catch.

The Dictator Designs a City

THE DICTATOR SITS alone in his underground bunker. The bunker is silent, despite the detonations and artillery fire tearing the streets overhead. The bunker is soundproof, permeable only to the classical music rustling from the speakers of a phonograph.

The dictator is designing a city worthy of imminent victory. Before he was a dictator, the dictator was an aspiring artist. His aspiration endured rejection by all the most prestigious art schools. He keeps his student portfolio—watercolor flowers, graphite landscapes, still lifes of fruit and statuary—in the false bottom of a file drawer dense with maps and memoranda housed in a cabinet lining one of the bunker's four walls.

He props the pads of his fingers gently along the edge of an enormous circular table. At either side, stacked boxes contain the city's landmarks in miniature: equestrian statues, triumphal arches, reticulated towers of gray glass, the domes of the legislature, the basin of a public fountain. Each piece was assembled by hand from the dictator's rigorous prototypes. He sorts the contents of each box. Soon, a forest grows along the table's circumference. Foliage spills onto the stage of the National Opera. He remembers the nativity scenes of his childhood, the tufts of straw he would arrange under wooden animals. He peers into a train car and is delighted to find a dozen cattle penned inside. He stands one upright on his hand; it rolls to one side, exposing rigid udders. He replaces it and reaches for another box. Anticipation turns to disappointment when the cover is removed. Figures for scale stare back at him from niches of insulating foam. There is a boy with a fishing pole, a girl with a tiny blonde doll pressed to her chest, an elderly woman hunched into the shape of her missing park bench. All civilians—the soldiers must be somewhere in the remaining stacks.

There are no windows in the dictator's bunker and all the regime's timepieces have been melted down for bullets. The only marker of time is the trickle of boxes from the table to the floor. Loose covers skim his ankles as miniatures accumulate in orderly radials.

He stops to rest at a vista of columns and masonry. He squints into the gap between buildings. The street vanishes into a satisfying distance. He proceeds to the next compass point. The opening here is broached by a lion's muzzle. From the west, a sliver of aqueduct; from the south a wedge of ascending marble steps. He moves to follow it, scraping his fingers on scrollwork and unyielding brick. He feels the missing piece, a cool pulsing against his skin. With bruised fingers, he traces its shape, framed neatly in the lines of his palm. As it begins to slip his grasp, he positions the chisel at his wrist to make the first incision.

Telephone

FED AT ONE end with facts, the town developed truisms. They paced the streets with little embellishment. The milkman was a milkman, pallid and bovine. The seamstress ate her meals stitch by stitch. The doctor's barbed cursive goaded moderation and exercise. It's just like that game, mused the gregarious grocer. You know the one I'm talking about? He barreled toward a waiting customer, trailing roughage from his feet.

ALICITA RODRÍGUEZ

How to Know You're a Woman
in a Junot Díaz Novel

THERE WILL BE mention of your ass. Your big ass. An ass so big it could alter the movement of the planets.

Sometimes it might be called your *culo*, which makes it more exotic.

Speaking of *culo*, expect to be machine-gunned by Spanglish, because you live in the *barrio*, where everyone's got to put their *medias* on before their *zapatos*.

You will like immature boys and violent men, especially nerdy types with small penises. Who knows why? You're not stupid.

Expect to be cheated on.

Expect to react dramatically with lots of colorful insults. You can't help it. You're fiery.

There will be tagging and chocolate factories.

There will be men who expect to be transformed by your vainglorious vagina—as if it could peel the skin off a mango.

But you will be punished for your power by being called *puerca* instead of Paula, *fea* instead of Felicia, and *sucia* instead of Sofia.

It's a small price to pay for "the alchemy of young pussy."

Negro, please.

How to Know You're a Woman
in a Kundera Novel

YOU ARE A wife or a mistress.

There is a good chance you have been raped—perhaps during the war. If you haven't, there's a good chance the men around you will have a shameful but violent desire to do so.

Blame it on the Prague Spring.

When a man says "Strip," you do as he says. Submission is intoxicating. Memorize that. It will come up often.

Everywhere, you hear discussions on art, music, and communism. Also, probes into the nature of love (sometimes *agape*—it's so deep). You get to speak, usually before or after sex. So much philosophy can make you forget your own subjugation.

You may be haunted by nightmares of cats scratching at your face.

Or one in which you are marched around a pool with a bunch of naked women, forced to sing cheerful songs.

You may participate in a threesome or an orgy. Alternatively, you might travel to an island and be raped by children. But you won't mind. Remember the Prague Spring?

Find comfort in the companionship of your dog.

How to Know You're a Woman
in a Murakami Novel

YOU WILL BE ghostly.

Being ghostly shouldn't bother you. The men who love you are also ghostly, disappearing in war and ennui and trains.

You will undoubtedly have sex with a boy or a young man suffering from undiagnosed depression, but it will be a simple act, not worth discussing later.

You probably have long black hair, but don't take it personally—it's Japan after all. And you get the dignity of having pubic hair. And you get to read and smoke cigarettes and wear glasses.

Perhaps you live in a netherworld, arrived at via a network of seemingly interminable hallways. Or through a well.

You will speak very little or ask too many questions, frustrating your love interest either way.

You might discover that there is another woman who eerily resembles you, possibly your twin. You should be happy you get a doppelganger.

On the other hand, you could end up in a sanatorium in Kyoto were they make you play basketball.

THADDEUS RUTKOWSKI

Cat's Teeth

WHEN I GOT home, I put my key in the lock and heard the sound of soft paws running toward me. I opened the metal door and saw my cat. When he got to me, he rubbed his back against my leg. I walked into the kitchen area and put food in a dish on the floor. I didn't watch him eat, but I could hear him huffing over the bowl.

I heard a knock on my front door and opened it. My downstairs neighbor was there—she had her dog on a leash. The dog was a large, energetic shepherd, and it wanted to come in. It reared back against its leash and beat at the air with its paws. It emitted loud panting sounds. My neighbor ruffled the fur on its neck, then put the dog in a headlock. "No!" she shouted. "No!"

I didn't know what my neighbor wanted. Whatever it was, it was probably trivial, something like a portion of sugar. But I didn't get to ask, because I'd forgotten about my cat. The sudden appearance of the dog alarmed him. The cat jumped onto my leg and latched on with his claws. He sank his teeth into my thigh and clamped down. His jaws were like the sides of a trap. He wouldn't, or couldn't, let go.

My neighbor dragged her dog away, and I kicked the cat off my leg. The cat didn't back off. He crouched as if he might spring again. I picked up a chair and held it in front of me, as if I were a lion tamer. I pointed the chair legs at the cat and thrust the piece of furniture forward. If I'd had a whip, I would have cracked it over my head. My cat looked like he'd gone wild. He'd gone back to the dawn of domestication.

The chair did the trick. The cat was cowed. He sank to the floor and eyed me. He looked like a tiny sphinx. His outburst was over.

During the uproar, my neighbor and her dog had disappeared.

I looked at my injury and saw four small wounds where the cat's incisors had sunk in. The punctures indicated a wide jaw opening, a large hinge in a feline mouth. This cat could eat a squirrel, if not a horse.

I heard my phone ring. It was my downstairs neighbor. "Sorry about that," she said, "but you should get your cat tested for rabies."

At night, I was alone with my cat, who appeared harmless now, sleeping in a coil, nose under a hind leg, his side rising and falling gently with the intake and outflow of air.

When I went to bed, I heard him scratching at the outside of my shut door. Then I heard him howling. Usually I ignored him, but on this night I opened the door. He came in quietly. At some point during the night, he came up onto the bed and slept with me.

MATTHEW SALESSES

Dear Estranger,

HERE ARE SOME things about Korea you never told me. They used to bury important people under giant mounds of earth. The old royal family is still alive and occupied the palace in Seoul *this* century. The Japanese occupiers dynamited the tops of mountains, killed all the tigers and tall people. Once, when the government needed to repay its debts, household after household turned in their personal family gold. My grandmother isn't buried, but burned, and her urn is in a glass display case with the same photo of her that you keep in your sock drawer and showed me once—you probably don't remember—the night you got drunk and told me I should go back to my mother, who was dead.

Your son

Dear Estranger,

TODAY I WENT to Gwangali Beach and watched couples hold each other. They aren't allowed to swim because it's the off-season—Korean laws are always trying to protect people from their desires. Do you ever think about what our family would have been like if you'd married my mother? I couldn't imagine you and her in any of the couples, because everyone was Korean. I am nearly as light as she was—that's what I got from her, tone. Would I be in Korea now if you had been my father my entire life? I didn't want to remember (but did anyway) the way white men looked at my white mother and me like she had been tainted and white women looked at us like I had been tainted. As a boy that was always when I imagined you beside us, not because I wanted you to stand up for her, but because I wanted to know how they would look at you. If you were here, in Korea, and she were still alive, and you two were married, would I feel at home here? Instead, I know what it is like to be made from a one-night stand, to be an exception. Whenever I go dancing I remember the risk of an exception becoming a life. You have made me a more careful person.

Your son

Dear Estranger,

IT TERRIFIES ME that if I taste something I've never tasted before, if I smell something I've never smelled before, if I see something I've never seen before, and like it—that my pleasure might tell me you would like it too. Yesterday I ate something straight out of the sea, from the flat of a blade, and it tasted like brine and fins and time. And I thought—time is what you would you think, too. Whatever squirmed in my mouth squirmed with an ancient dignity. How preposterous to it that I, a bastard, was eating it. How could you and I be from the same genes—is more something you would say. But is that the question that has brought me to Korea? What terrifies me most is the possibility that what makes a man drop everything and move to a country he's never been to before is about his father, not himself. Maybe this is a false dichotomy. Maybe a false dichotomy should be our mascot.

Your son

Translation Folio

DENISE EMMER

Translator's Introduction

DENISE EMMER IS A UNIQUE presence in Brazilian letters (and would be unique, for that matter, in other countries' literary stables). She studied physics and cello performance while at the Federal University of Rio de Janeiro. Then she did post-graduate work in philosophy. She also made several records of popular music, including *Pelos Caminhos da America* (1981) and *Canto Lunar* (1984). One of her songs "Alouette" sold over 300 thousand copies and earned her a gold record. She has recorded soundtrack music for tele-novelas and currently plays cello for the Camerata Dias Gomes in Rio. In Brazil she may be better known as a musician because of her early success as an MPB (Musica Popular Brasileira) musician. In this manner she follows in the tradition of other Brazilian poets.

Several Brazilian poets through several generations are as well known for their lyrics set to music as they are for their verse set down on the page in books. The first of these is Manuel Bandeira, whose lyrics/poems were set to music in the 20's by Heitor Villa-Lobos and have become standards much in the way that the songs of Tin Pan Alley have become standards. Song/poems like "Modinha" and "Danza" from Bachianas Brasileiras No. 5 have been covered by many MPB stars and opera singers. Also Bandeira wrote the lyrics for the charmingly simple and nationally renowned "Azulão," composed by Jaime Ovalle (a good friend of Villa-Lobos), which is part of the operatic repertoire as well as a song that children sing in school (imagine Renee Fleming singing "Pop Goes the Weasel" in a concert hall).

Another well-known poet who is also known just as much for his musical contributions as his literary ones is Vinicius de Moraes. He is probably best known for a plethora of hits during the golden age of bossa nova—"Felicidade" and "Garota da Ipanema (The Girl from Ipanema)," just to name a few that Antonio Carlos Jobim composed. However, Vinicius de Moraes also teamed up with Toquinho, a bossa nova guitarist. In the 1970s with Vinicius often straddling the line between talking and singing, the two of them enjoyed a recording career that saw them land several hits and many beloved songs.

However, Denise Emmer is different from those above in the respect that she is not just the lyricist or (in the case of Vinicius) a singer. She is truly a musician as well as the composer of the lyrics. On her last record entitled *Capote das Pedras* (*Cloak of Stones*) she plays guitar and piano and sings. On the record one of the songs is "Pontos Cardeias" ("Cardinal Directions"), which is also a poem in her most recent book *Poema Cenário e Outros Silêncios* (*Landscape Poem and Other Silences*). She also covers "Dizer Adeus (Say Farewell)," a poem by countryman, friend and poet Ivan Junqueira. Add to this the fact that she also plays cello in several chamber groups throughout Rio, and you have a biography that is truly unique among poets.

Her literary side is equally diverse. She has published seventeen books—three novels, the rest poems. From 1987 to 2009 she won a number of prizes, including some the most prestigious awards in Brazil. Most of her work resides firmly within the surrealist tradition. Her images are carefully crafted to be evocative, and often they provide political commentary through their connotation. This places her work more in the vein of surrealist writing like Aimé Cesaire; however, stylistically her work is quite different than his. She does not work with an expansive and rambling palette as in Cesaire's "Notebook of a Return to the Native Land." Her work is usually very much the work of a formalist, unusual for the surrealist who is often invoking the wild and the visionary and the strange. Emmer's lines are much better behaved and probably earn this kind of treatment because of her experience as a songwriter, where end rhymes mark the completion of a musical phrase. You can see this kind of strict adherence to rhyme scheme in "Noite Maga" where the *abba* rhyme scheme is apparent, a stylistic move unlike that of more freewheeling surrealists.

I have chosen not to reflect this formalism in my translations mainly because recreating the rhymes in English is nearly impossible to do without making them sound forced. The most striking thing about Emmer's work is her image play. Early on in her poems of the 1980s [*Cançoes de Acender a Noite* (*Songs of the Lit Up Night*) and *Equaçáo da Noite* (*Night Equation*)] this imagery focuses intensely on astronomical subjects, a kind of cosmic surrealism. In this work the night sky appears as the stage on which all of Emmer's concerns play. Later work shifts its focus onto more worldly matters, such as the aforementioned concern with national and international politics, and more recently onto her interest in rock climbing (as seen in "Diário de Vôo") as well as an ongoing interest in matters of the heart and love and her dedication to her parents, the lionized writers (of telenovelas and other works) Janete Clair and Dias Gomes. Novelist Rachel de Queiróz has aptly described her images as "extremely personal, inventive, refashioned, exciting, and absurdly unexpected and magical." Certainly her brand of surrealism is sparse and crisp, yet somehow it retains the feel of the supernatural.

Denise Emmer belongs to that tradition of Brazilian musician poets who seamlessly fuse these two areas—poetry and music—that are generally held separate in American literature, and she does this in a way that satisfies both musicians and poets. Her music is sufficiently complex in its composition and instrumentation that it does not strike one as danceable pablum, and her written work holds up on the page among poet/songwriters to a degree that perhaps even exceeds that of Leonard Cohen. Her work represents a marriage of these two art forms and expresses the manner in which poetry can break out of the solely "literary" bubble. In a country where poetry quite literally has had currency—Carlos Drummond de Andrade's "Canção

Amiga" ("Friendly Song") was printed on the old 50 Cruzados bill—Emmer's work reaches across the boundaries of the art forms of music and literature in ways that are not readily permitted for American poets.

To the Night

The night is inebriated
and will dance in space
wearing the costume of the birds
flying into the infinite

I open the world's window
and don't I already see your face
carrying the lake of the moon
to the great festival of the waters

where another dawn
hides itself in your mirror

in the corners where I can't see
the night changing its path of flight?

Flight Notes

In the distance I see my father flying
In his aerial cathedral
Writing down his ethereal missions
For many little rebellions.

And then the clouds change
Themselves into his dark horses
And turn his silent robes
Into the architecture of his figure

He rolls up the sleeves
Of his immaterial shirt
He fires off a profane film
To agitate the abyss

God streams in through windows
The monks creak in their graves
My father keeps pressing his attack
—his dialogue with Thanatos.

Movement

for Germano

I arrive at port in your arms
The undulating hill
Your pulsing quasar
Unsettles my lap

The sound of the compasses
Of earth's flames
Leads us into war
Toward the bright blades

Transporting me in your ships
with their toy masts
is like a story plot
with legs and the incoming tide

The Laws of Archimedes
Apply to the sound of a thrust
Love does not realize
That no one owns blood.

Night of the Witch

I walked with you on the dunes
On the pages of sand
I thought about distant sirens
But they were grave and serious schooners

And questioning who you were
The sea moved its ships
They seemed like estrous mares
female animals flying without a saddle

Then they began to die
On the road with the velvet hand
That lifted me up and placed me among
the deaf in the tenuous dawn

The separation of kiss and indulgence
The smell of leaf and rain
Your smile beyond the curve
At the point of the precipice

The night of the witch runs far away
Into its strange palace
I can't decipher your dream
that populates my waters.

Translated from the Portuguese by Tim Kahl

YERRA SUGARMAN

Sunday Aubade: A Faithful Remix

For me, there was no lingerie glitzy as stars,
but I'd wear the nylon nets of dime-store pantyhose and loved
the fragile bowl of your pelvis sheltered in flannel pajamas.

And it was good to wake up to a sky loosened
from the dark, to the whip-poor-wills and bobolinks
shooting up and up, jabbing the wind.

Good to wake up to your belly quivering like a sleeping cat;
to the mayhem of sheets; to the burning
sunlight on your thighs; to the slope

of your slim fingers, the dawn between them, its pink
clouds like feathers. Good to wake up to your hips' cursive;
to your unfastened lips; to your ribs so delicate they'd once broken

when you coughed. To our blouses tangled on the floor;
to our shoes lined up against the screen-door,
mud hardened on them. You were teaching me to purge

the bad hemoglobin of youthful madness, to *offer it up*
and give it over to what's larger than the self,
until what we *offered up* was this secret

way we'd discovered out of womb and wound.
But love is a kind of madness,
although, as Socrates understood, it is good.

To lose one's mind, he said, is the path toward finding it.
It is good to remember the moment I'd awaken to your skin
coursing from your shoulders into tributaries

of shadow and you still the pilot of my maddening body.

JENNY MOLBERG

The Disembodied Woman

The first time was at summer camp.
Nine years old, I wet the bed.
I washed the sheets in the moonlit sink,

hung them in the blue light, the rocked path
needling my bare feet. I didn't cry
but wrung my clothes in the showers,

tucked a blanket into the corners of my bunk
like I'd seen my mother do, and watched
the dawn lift over the small mountain

as a girl rising from childhood. I held my hurt
like a stone in my throat. Now, it is myself
I try to hold as a stone.

When I breathe in the mossy scent
of my dog's stilled body, I am veiled in fur
and the ceiling of my homesickness bears down

like a white shroud. Metamorphic, I am feldspar.
I am an ion with itchy feet and so I ramble
and sometimes I cannot find my own hands.

I once read of a woman much like me
who woke without her hands. First her hands,
then her jaw, her back, her legs . . .

until her whole body was no longer hers.
She had to learn to see herself again.
O stone, help me remember.

As I walk with the dog into the woods
this morning, I think I recognize
my own wandering gaze in her cataracted eyes.

I touch my shoulders, my hips. I bend
to cup my knees. As the trees magnify their gaze,
I make what looks like a prayer:

the barks curls forward—so many
wooden ears. Someone is whispering
these are my hands, these are my hands.

LUANNE CASTLE

What Came Between a Woman and Her Duties

14 May 1897

On this Friday, in our fair city of Kalamazoo, Recreation Park refreshment proprietor, John Culver, has applied to the Circuit Court to gain custody of his two young daughters from his divorced wife. The girls currently reside in the Children's Home. They were accompanied to court by Miss Bradley, the matron of the home.

Mrs. Culver, the divorcée, and the children were represented by J. W. Adams. The father was represented by F.E. Knappen. Mrs. Culver, pale and stern-looking, wore a shirtwaist with tightly ruched collar and generous mutton sleeves. The strain of her situation shows clearly on her visage. In the past, Mrs. Culver has been aided and abetted by her female friends in the art of painting, as an article of 6 February 1895 in this very daily can attest.

A large number of friends of both parties were in the courtroom and heard emotional pleadings on both sides. Judge Buck ascertained that Mrs. Culver is engaged in the pursuit of an honest living at this time and so ordered that the children remain in the mother's care. She was given six months to bring them home from the orphanage or they will go into the care of their father and his mother. Let us hope that Mrs. Culver can stay away from the easel.

JACOB BOYD

The Substitute's History of the Holy Trumpet

I.

I've lost the class. These girls. So sworn to the door, to the glitter-and-cursive-nerve of these halls. Fidgeting beneath shelves of pickled shrew and stuffed, dusty, mite-eaten owls. Sighing like furnaces. What song could convince them to articulate the bones now laid before them? What tempo and level of heartbreak?

II.

The starlet of the soccer squad teases an anchor across the coast of her breastbone. This four-line section is her shoreless sea. The hour, in wormlike complicity, digs its minutes into her skin. Tiny rowers and spores fight to mount her waist without the least clue what they're climbing toward. Her nails, tarred with paint, confuse and wave.

III.

Though I have felt eternal, I feel small and outpaced. Let them text. Let them turn from science to the flagpole's asymmetric tolling, a brass clip clanging against a pole. Its one note enlarges our silence. Have you heard the fanfare of docked sailboats on a windy, rainy day? The bell sends us streaming like bats out of the room.

IV.

Day two. I show them a comic I saw this morning. A butterfly, emerging from chrysalis, flies straight into a spider web. Stuck, the unlucky insect squeaks: *Goddamn it*. I log on and we stream the eagle's nest. Root for the doomed runt. In comes the fish, in comes the rabbit, in comes the mouse. The eaglets open their mouths.

ESTHER LIN

I See Her Best

when she's half-hidden.
As if my eyelids were mother's skirts.
When there's darkness like a kerosene lamp's.
Hair glossy as a catfish flank.
A lone woman released from China
to join her fiancé in Vietnam.
When abandoned, seducing a married man.
When cast out, crossing borders,
a silent river raft in purple twilight.
To meet my father, for the first time.
He—more beautiful than she.
When split by cancer, asking my father
and her new lover to pray together.
Red Guard. Red tape.
What facts. What luck.
A Xeroxed photo in my desk.
1974. A young woman clasping the arm
of a married man, her wrapped hair
and secret smile, her face, or a version of the face
I touch in my sleep. I don't claim anything.
Not because I don't believe in ways of survival,
but my imagination is small.
Metastasis and blood count.
They don't say *disembowel*, but that's what they did.
Colostomy. Hysterectomy.
A legal miracle, my history professor said
of the flight from China. *Millions starving,
and your mother gets married.*

ANDREW GRACE

from the Last Will and Testament of Said Gun

My mother was thrown by a horse into a ditch. She was not thirty. My father re-saddled the beast that killed his wife and used him to till. Whatever grudge he bore he strewed like black crumbs across the woods of my childhood.

As I grew older, my mother became a theory about memory and the self: what if I remembered more about gray wolves than my own mother? What part wolf was I, what part her, or was the ghost of my mother my mother?

And whose snarl did I store in my throat for safekeeping? Who laid a pelt of light over my skinny bed as I slept?

Smoked corn silks and threw rocks at the pigs.

Urinated on our property line to ward off strangers.

Jerked off thinking about the motion of trains, the hot stink of iron, the relentless pumping forward a model of abnegating the present I loved deeply.

Untied pasture fences.

Stole diesel with my siphon mouth.

Stared in horror at a drying line of bras.

Walked widely across the acres that ran flatly to the horizon.

Became my own blood brother.

Just existing was my revelation.

Shot holes in grain silos, watched them piss corn.

Hunted grubs, foxes, quarters, raccoons, tree tops, nudity, quails, owls, nicotine, bullets, ewes, nails, fish, knowledge concerning vaginas, rabbits, baseballs, newts, rainbows, razorblades, things smaller than me weeping.

Forgave my own sins by feeding bits of fat on the end of a stick to repulsive hatchlings.

I didn't realize I lived in the middle of nowhere. "Middle" implies being between two things, and as everything surrounding me was so endless, I didn't imagine it ever stopped. "Nowhere" implies a somewhere: buildings, commerce, density. I thought America meant the largest stall in the dairy barn. I thought the fourth of July celebrated the corn rising above my head. I thought the fireworks my father lit were a lesson teaching me to look up, as the horizontal world would be gone until October. I didn't realize I lived "in" a place in the context of other places. The landscape was so precise: the whirr of a cow's intake of breath, the warm smell of soy and the cold smell of tar, ice on an eyelash, a squirrel trickling down an oak like a bead of sweat. Did "I" "live"? The landscape thought and I watched.

We had a cream separator, corn-shelling machine, 2 kerosene lamps, wood-burning stove that was often fed corncobs, a radio. Three quarters of a tractor. A three-point hitch. A Go-Dig. A barn for the cows, two horses, a black-tarred pig shed, a coop, a tool closet and a house.

Our house had a view of other men's land in all directions but East, which was ours. 80 acres. Mother had decorated it, and in a rare flair for the exotic, she chose for the kitchen wallpaper a pattern featuring large red cranes. There were three figures: one of the bird staring at its reflection in a pond, one of it of spreading its wings to take off, and lastly the crane in full flight position, legs trailing, head retracted into the body. As a boy I would spin around in the center of the kitchen and create a moving picture of the crane, frozen, launching, taking flight, over and over.

The posture of the crane in the pond seemed to express fear at what he saw in the water. Its flight seemed to be an attempt to escape from what frightened him. What he saw was himself. He escapes. And he is looking at a red face in the water.

ERIN KATE RYAN

Half-Lives of Sisters

MY SISTER IS A DIFFERENT person since the accident. A jack-knifed semi, the old Camaro she was in, and everybody else dead. Two and a half weeks in the hospital. They shaved her head to drill into her skull and release the pressure on her brain.

Aunt Cathy used to call us, me and Karen, the *tow-headed twosome*. My sister's not tow-headed anymore; she's been keeping her head shaved since she came back. I help her sometimes, but mostly just watch. My sister used to be four years older than me, but now I think there's five or six years between us.

The accident knocked all of us off our rockers. That's another Aunt Cathy thing to say. For a while after coming back from the hospital, my sister couldn't remember my name or which bedroom door was hers. She called me Bud instead of Jake, which eventually I decided was okay. Mom cried for a week straight and Dad walked around like one of my video game zombies, forgetting his tie and going to the office in his lawn-cutting clothes. Aunt Cathy basically moved in and took over. She made me do chores, which Mom and Dad never did, and was really strict about me playing my game at the dinner table. Mom eventually came back to herself, thank god, and started talking back to Aunt Cathy, finally telling her to go home to her own apartment. I'd been trying real hard since the night of the accident to rack up as many extra lives as I could to be ready for the zombie armageddon. Once Aunt Cathy left it got a lot easier.

I can get kind of obsessive over them, my lives, and when I can I hit pause on the game and save it right before I do something hard. That way if I die, I can reset and go back to where I saved like nothing ever happened and my life count stays the same.

Before the accident, Karen was all set to go to boarding school for senior year, this artsy place in Michigan for kids who got in trouble a lot or else were actors, and she'd been practically packed since the acceptance letter came. Aunt Cathy was going to help Mom and Dad pay. Aunt Cathy didn't approve of the way Mom and Dad were raising me and Karen, and she was the one in the family who had some money, so she got to give her opinion whenever she wanted.

Around the time Mom told Aunt Cathy to leave, my sister unpacked every last box and I tossed the cardboard onto the recycling for her, since her left arm was still in a sling. When I ask her now if she's ever going to move out, she just says, "Give me a minute, okay?"

Before the accident, Karen was a lefty and drew a shirtsleeve tattoo all the way up to her right shoulder in Sharpie every week. Her best was the Virgin de Guadeloupe, which she copied from a t-shirt that I bought her for Christmas two years ago from the skate shop. After a year, there were pores on her upper arm that were permanent ghosts of the Virgin's cape. The ghosts disappeared after the hospital.

My sister's right-handed now. After she was out of the sling, she tried drawing the Virgin on her right arm anyway, over the real tattoo of a bluebird that was already there, but the drawing was wobbly, more ghost than Virgin, and we could all still see what was underneath. We pretended not to see, though, just like we pretended not to see the other stuff, like the color of her eyes and the crookedness of her teeth. Anyway, she wore long sleeves most of the time so it was easy.

The whole family goes to my sister's follow-up appointments and we stand facing the doctors like an army, *a united front*, Aunt Cathy says. At the last one, I accidentally said something about how Karen was left-handed before the accident. The doctor's face got all pinched. "With any brain trauma there's—" he said. "And with the sling—"

The doctor wasn't as good a prentender as we'd turned out to be. We could make anything make sense since the accident.

"Karen's always been ambidextrous," Mom said.

After the doctor's, we drove through McDonald's and then went home to chill out, *have family time*, Mom said. Dad took the rest of the day off, and we sat all four of us on the sofa, me and my sister between Mom and Dad, and watched a bunch of old family comedies. Mom had both arms wrapped around my sister almost the whole time, only unwrapping one of them when Aunt Cathy called to see how the appointment went.

I played my zombie game on mute during the movies, though I did try to look like I was happy to be sitting there with everybody. I was up to 632 lives by then but the phone ringing made me accidentally walk off a cliff without saving the game first. The ticker clocked down to 631 as I started the level again and for the first time ever I started thinking about where those extra lives came from, and whether they'd been somebody else's to begin with and what it meant, then, that I was taking over somebody else's life to fight zombies.

My sister's not the same person since the accident. The truck driver and her friend Jaz dead, and her now right-handed, brown-eyed, and broader in the shoulders. That Guadeloupe t-shirt doesn't fit her anymore.

On the night of the accident, my whole family was sitting in the hospital waiting room for about forever and a half, knowing a whole lot of nothing. It was the police who came out first and told us about the semi and that Jaz and the truck driver were dead, and that it probably wasn't Jaz's fault, that she was maybe speeding a little but that there was no way she could have seen the semi before she came over the hill to stop in time. The Camaro was in pieces, they said. Actual little burned-up pieces, like a special effect in the movies. Dad asked if they'd called Jaz's mom and they said they'd left several messages but no one had called back.

Karen wasn't supposed to hang out with Jaz because she had no adult supervision, Mom said, and Jaz's mom was bad news, according to Aunt Cathy. Before the rule about not hanging out, Karen and Jaz used to spend a lot of time in the kitchen and they talked like I couldn't hear them, even though I was just in the living room. Jaz called her mom The Fish and was always telling some story about The Fish leaving an answering machine message from a hotel room in Toledo or Chicago, and then rolling back into town three or four days after she said she was going to. It didn't sound so bad to me. All afternoon, Jaz would pound back pixie sticks, dozens of them in a go, and Karen would wrap the empty wrappers around her fingers like she was a boxer.

This one night before the accident, the manager of some pizza place called to tell Mom and Dad that Karen and Jaz were stoned and making trouble, knocking tables over and throwing popcorn around the restaurant. Mom drove over there to yank Karen home by the elbow (no one came for Jaz and eventually the manager just let her go) and in the car on the way home they got into it at a stoplight and Karen twisted in her seat and pulled back her left elbow and punched Mom in the face. Because of the punch, Mom rear-ended the car sitting at the light in front of them and the cops came and Mom lied and held her palm to her cheek and said her foot slipped for no reason.

That night, Mom sat on the sofa with a bag of peas on her face and cried real ugly and hiccuppy, and asked Karen through the peas, "Why why why must you make me your enemy?" Karen just kind of laughed and said, "Grounded, right?" then went upstairs and locked her bedroom door and called Jaz. Mom sat and cried with Dad until after I was in bed with my iPad. "Is this it for us? Is this the only relationship I get with my daughter?" Over and over again like it was the end of the world. I started to get why Karen had walked away.

It was after the punch and the rear-ending (which we called "the accident" until the big accident that changed everything) that Mom and Dad told Karen she couldn't hang out with Jaz anymore. Jaz was older and she'd already dropped out of high school and drove her busted-out Camaro around the subdivision in the afternoons. From soccer practice I could see her doing figure eights around the blocks of ranch houses, waiting for Karen to finish up at rehearsal or detention, the two places you used to reliably be able to find her. Despite what Mom and Dad said, Karen got in Jaz's car almost every day, and a lot of the time Jaz let her drive, even though Karen wasn't even allowed to get her learner's permit till graduation.

My sister freaked out a little when Dad mentioned signing her up for driver's ed now that she'll be living here instead of at boarding school. Dad said it like he wasn't thinking, wasn't really even looking at her, just stood there holding the car insurance bill and opened his mouth like he was just talking out some train of thought from before the accident. When she started crying, saying "What? No. No. No," Dad went real red and he let his hands fall to the table and he said, "Fuck," which he never says in front of us. I went and sat down next to my sister and held her hand.

"Actually, let's just stick to bikes for now," Mom said. "When the vertigo's passed, when you're up for it." Her hand was on Dad's arm. "You've got a bike, Karen," she said. "It's in the garage. Jake can show you. It's green. You know, green. And has white tires. Right, Jake? Right, Bud?"

Since my sister's not going to art school anymore, Mom and Dad registered her for private school in town. "A fresh start," Mom said.

"Unprecedented," Aunt Cathy said, sliding the tuition check into an envelope.

Before the accident, I didn't know much about Jaz and I didn't really think about her. She was Old Neighborhood, part of the twenty-ish families that have basically lived and died here for a hundred years. Aunt Cathy knew The Fish really well—they were tight back when they were teenagers—and remembers when The Fish left high school from being knocked up. (Karen once said it was Aunt Cathy's boyfriend who did it, which is why she never got married. I think it's probably why Aunt Cathy seemed to hate Jaz and is so uneasy around my sister since the accident, but saying it out loud would make me anti-feminist. And there's also really no one for me to say a thing like that to, anyway.) My bedroom shares a wall with Karen's, and back before the accident I could hear her and Jaz on the phone till real late, Karen saying things like, "Shush shush," like she was rocking a baby doll, and, "She's a fucking monster." I remember one night when I heard Karen at three a.m., after her cell phone woke me up, saying, "Shit, Jaz, you gotta get out of there." The next morning, Jaz came out of Karen's bedroom real early, before Dad's alarm clock even went off. I was awake though, and I heard a crick outside my door and peeked through the crack. Jaz didn't see me see her, tight red jeans all scrunched at her knees, blue-black hair but red at the roots, bird tattoo, purple bruise on her cheek, and the smell of body and cigarettes.

Mom and Jaz got in a fight one time, really going at each other. I'd never seen Mom's nasty side pop out when company was around. Mom came home while Karen and Jaz were sitting at the kitchen table rolling cigarettes in pixie sticks wrappers—Jaz definitely wasn't even allowed in the house then—and started using that short, hard voice she has when she's mad but trying to stay calm, like turning a screwdriver too hard against a screw, asking Karen why she'd skipped out on school that afternoon, why she was so cavalier with her future, why she couldn't take better care in choosing her friends. Mom actually said that right in front of Jaz. "Some people will just swallow you whole if you let them," she said, real mean, like she was jealous of them.

Cavalier is one of those Aunt Cathy words that she uses when she and Mom argue about their lives and the way Mom and Dad raise their kids. Aunt Cathy used it again after the accident when Mom came back to herself and told Aunt Cathy to go back to her own home. *Cavalier* and *playing with fire*.

On that day before the accident, the one with the cigarette and pixie sticks wrappers, Jaz stood up and started packing up her stuff while Karen was yelling at Mom, "You are such a cunt! How can you say shit like that?"

Cunt was one of the words that Karen told me was anti-feminist to say, when she'd sometimes give me these speeches about how I should treat women, even though she was mostly talking about herself and not me.

"Listen, lady," Jaz said, sounding real calm next to Karen. "Your kid didn't choose her friends. I chose her. I'm her only fucking friend, and if you think that's tragic, then fuck you."

"I won't tolerate being talked to that way," Mom said.

"Seems like there's not much that you do tolerate," Jaz yelled back, slamming her bag against the table and knocking a bunch of glasses and bottles over. A half liter of Coke fell on its side and soda started pulsing out of the spout. I zoomed into the kitchen and rescued my iPad from the table before it got sticky or fried.

Jaz left then, and Karen, crying and screaming at the same time, called Mom an effing monster. "Why are you so determined for me to have no friends?" she shouted.

"Think about what your choice of friends says about you, my dear," Mom said. "Is that who you want to be?" The soda dripped onto Karen's big black Harley Davidson boots while the two of them stood there hating each other. Before the accident, Karen's feet were huge. It was one of our favorite family jokes when we were both little, Karen's Bozo-sized sneakers. "Where did that giant raccoon come from?" Dad would ask with a fakey horrified voice. "Oh, nevermind, it's just Karen's slipper."

For the first few weeks after my sister came home from the hospital, she basically lived in sweat pants. After she unpacked all the art school boxes, she started weeding through the clothes in the closet, tossing out the stuff that reminded me most of Karen: the leggings with the zippers, the plaid strappy tops, the skirt she'd made from a Misfits t-shirt, the Virgin of Guadeloupe shirt, all the art supplies and Smiths CDs. Mom stood and watched while my sister tossed this stuff with her one good arm—the other still in the sling—into the hallway. Mom didn't say a lot, but when my sister was done and she stood up straight, all red in the face and a little sweaty on her bald head, Mom said, "Tomorrow we'll go get some new stuff, okay?"

My mom hasn't been the same since the accident. She's been really quiet, and gets wet in the eyes lots of times every day. She acts a little shy around my sister, like you can see her muscles deciding whether it's okay to reach out and touch her shoulder. The girl who's my sister now always seems happy to be touched, though. She hugs Mom and Dad constantly, and she scruffles at my hair basically every time I see her. She's stiffer around Aunt Cathy, though, real polite. She's getting better from the accident, and moving through the house more easily. For a while, she was stumbling a lot in those gigantic Harley Davidson boots, but Aunt Cathy showed up one day with some size-medium yellow slip-on sneakers from Old Navy.

Aunt Cathy can drive you nuts, but she's good at sizing up what you need.

Since the accident, my sister's shorter than she was and her bald-head stubble grows in reddish. She wears the boring clothes my mom bought her at the department store and lets Aunt Cathy wrap floaty floral scarves around her head to hide the scar from the drill that made a hole in her skull. She hugs the family and she shakes every time she gets into a car and she laughs at old movies like it's the first time she's ever seen them.

Every so often I wish I could talk to Karen. Before the accident, Karen and I hardly talked at all except when she was giving me the feminist lecture or when she was grounded and pissed off at Mom and Dad. If my sister was the same as before the accident, though, I might memorize some jokes about the hole in her head and her brains leaking out and how she should avoid anywhere zombies were known to congregate. I can't say that stuff now, though. My sister who came home from the hospital talks to me more, asking about soccer and what I'm playing on my iPad, but she's real sensitive about everything and it seems like it'll be years and years before I can make fun of her about anything. So I tried to teach her my game, how you get to pick your player and change their strengths and what they look like, except she still has vertigo from the accident, especially when looking at screens or words. She tried a few turns, but she just kept losing lives since she couldn't really see. She handed it back to me. "Here, be me," she said. "You're better."

Every so often I want to ask the girl who's my sister now about what happened the night of the accident. I want to ask her about the extra lives in the zombie game, whether she thinks that each new life is taking over the last, and whether hitting save before dying is basically a cheat. I want to offer her pixie sticks and make sure she knows I understand that it's complicated. I want to ask her about the bird tattoo and a bunch of other stuff, except that if I do she might be afraid to stop shaving her head or being good all the time.

Before the accident, when Karen got into art school it was the battle of the century. She hadn't even told Mom and Dad she was applying. "Seventeen years old and acts like she has any clue," Mom said at least once a day in that stripped-screw voice. Dad, who generally tries not to have big opinions on anything about us kids, said to Mom that maybe this was a way of keeping Karen away from Jaz. I think Karen heard him say that, because she started playing it up real big, wearing Jaz's ID bracelet to the table, texting her during dinner, pulling all the way into the driveway in Jaz's car instead of stopping around the corner like she had before. She even started kissing Jaz right on the lips whenever she got out of the car, opening the car door so the dome light came on before she did it.

Then Aunt Cathy offered to help with tuition and suddenly Karen was packing boxes.

My sister is different since the accident, and yesterday I finally asked her if she misses her before-accident life. "No way," she said, and she did the scruffle thing on my head with her left hand, now out of the sling. "Stuff is great now, right?"

"Do you miss the before-accident Karen?" I asked.

My sister looked at me for forever and a half. "Do you?" she asked me back. "There wasn't a big sibling thing happening before the accident, was there?"

"Sure," I said, and I turned on my iPad. "But I think you can miss something even if it wasn't that great." I zapped a zombie with my destroyer ray. I was still using my sister's player and I'd racked up a bunch of lives for her, too. I said, "I don't think it's right just to forget."

Now that my sister wears yellow sneakers and floaty scarves like she's Mom and Aunt Cathy's idea of Miss American Pie, I snagged the Virgin of Guadeloupe shirt and Karen's sketchbooks and pencils that were boxed up with the other clothes to head to the Salvation Army. I've been practicing drawing the Virgin and copying some of Karen's other sketches, although most of them were of Jaz. I know it's not my job to be Karen, or who she might have been without the accident or anything, but it's just not okay to give her up completely. On the top shelf of Mom and Dad's closet is the plastic tub where all the photos of before-accident Karen live now. I pulled out one of my favorites from last year, Karen giving the camera the finger, and worked on altering some of Karen's drawings of Jaz to look more like Karen used to. I'm real careful with the pencil, just sketching in lightly until I can get better at it. I've got this idea that I can balance stuff out, somehow, if I keep at it. It's the same reason, I think, that Aunt Cathy got Jaz's old ID bracelet from the nurse at the hospital and gave it to my sister. Me with Karen's sketchbooks, my sister with the ID bracelet, Mom with my sister, Aunt Cathy with Mom.

The night of the accident, right at the start of summer, the phone rang at home around midnight and Mom just started going, "What. What?" My dad was sitting right there, kind of sleeping and watching Fox News at the same time, but he woke up when Mom's voice got all serious—she wasn't even shouting, it was just the way that everything dropped out and she sounded like hollow plastic, like an empty milk jug. I could hear this all from my room even though I wasn't supposed to be awake playing my game, and when Dad came in I sat up real quick. "We're going to the hospital," he said. "Your sister. Shoes. Jacket."

We were waiting at the admission desk and no one was telling us anything. Mom had her screwdriver voice on and Dad was still sounding asleep when he talked to the nurse behind the desk. I was holding my iPad but felt kind of like playing games would make everyone mad.

My sister doesn't know the part of the accident story where the police came out and told us that Jaz's mom had never called them back—at least, she doesn't know it from us. Mom skips it whenever she talks about that night. It's hard to imagine that my sister hasn't figured it out, though.

After the accident, I saw my sister going through Mom's yearbook, looking at the girls who were in Aunt Cathy's class. The photos were black and white, but you could still tell somehow that one of the girls was a redhead. Like that old TV show of Aunt

Cathy's, the one that's black and white but is all about a lady being a redhead and a troublemaker. Somehow you can just tell by looking at her. And with my sister's head shaved, I could see the resemblance, when I went back later and looked. I got a little caught up on that part, looking at that old photo of The Fish from before she became such a terrible mom and then lost her daughter altogether, trying to figure out if it's okay to lose something you treated so bad to begin with.

The doctor let us in, finally. She had started to wake up.

The doctors had already shaved off her hair because of the brain swelling thing, and her face was covered with deep blue bruises and there was black makeup on her cheeks and under her eyes. Her curled-up feet were tiny biscuits under the blanket, and you could just see the blue-black tip of a beak under the short sleeve of her hospital johnny. There was a clear plastic plug in her mouth that the nurse said was a breathing tube. "She can't talk yet," the nurse said.

We all stood there for forever and a half. A ticking sound came from down in Mom's throat every so often and Dad was leaning white-handed onto the rail at the foot of the bed. The hospital machines made hospital machine noises. On the tray next to the bed was a plastic bag that had "Patient's Personal Effects" printed on it in orange, real big like it was trying too hard. It had a pair of red jeans, a black jean jacket I'd never seen before, and some checkered Chucks that were stained a really dark brown. What it didn't have was a wallet or ID bracelet or a pile of sketchbooks or a t-shirt that was a present from her little brother or anything that made a person a person.

In my zombie game, every so often there's a moment when I come up to something completely impossible, like a fifty-foot brick wall and a hundred zombies on their way to eat my brains. It usually takes me dying seven or twelve times before I realize that I can use the flower pot from level four and the truncheon from level five to get up and over the wall and divert the zombies into the ocean. The moment when it all comes together and everything happens like I suddenly saw that it could is a perfect, maybe even indescribable, moment. It's not even that I feel so great about myself for figuring it out; it's more like I feel lucky to get to witness everything that came before it and how there's this convergence of just the right stuff and situation. Usually it's so awesome and I've got so much adrenaline that it doesn't matter how many times I died getting there and Dad tells me to stop shouting for Chrissakes it's after eleven.

Basically, though, it means I had already figured it all out when, after a million years, Mom started fussing with the bed covers and checking the chart. "Do you think she's warm enough?" she whispered to Dad, and she started looking around the room and in the closets until she found another blanket. It was even a little exciting, everything coming together just like that, and Mom's voice rose to her regular Mom-volume, although it wasn't exactly her regular voice. And Dad got it real fast, too, and then all three of us were taking care of that girl in the bed, my sister in the bed, because that's what your family does. And Aunt Cathy walked into the room and we all faced her like an army, a united front, and told her to keep her voice down so that she wouldn't wake up my sister. And we did it with all that adrenaline and of course I didn't even think then about how playing my sister's player in the game doesn't really mean that it's her who's surviving the zombie attack. How winning new lives doesn't really make up for losing them.

Every so often I want to talk to my sister about that time in the hospital room. I want to ask the girl who's my sister now about the look she had on her face when she opened her eyes to a squint and saw the four of us standing there—Mom who was so mean to her, me and Dad and Aunt Cathy who basically she barely knew, us four holding all the stuff about her life, knowing that her best friend had been driving the car, that her best friend was dead, that she, there in the hospital bed, was the only person left alive. Us four holding the impossible idea of a brand new life. Unprecedented, Aunt Cathy would say.

Her, not being able to talk with the tube in her throat, that big bandage on the back of her bald head looking like maybe she *had* survived a zombie attack, actually. Not being able to ask a question or choke or cough when, after forever and a half, my mom stepped toward her and said, "Karen, sweetheart, it's us."

AIMÉE BAKER

Wretched Women

Wretched and deluded woman! In vain was the foul and unnatural murder committed under the protecting shade of night, in your lone and sequestered dwelling, where no human eye was near to witness your guilt.

—Judge Rueben Walworth, at the sentencing of Peggy Facto who was convicted of murdering her newly born child in 1825 in Plattsburgh, NY

MY DAUGHTER IS A STUDY in light. White blonde hair that hangs wild down her back, so long it touches her sixth vertebra. Her body soaked in it, her skin moonstone white and reflective. And that skin, barely touched by the sun, still baby soft even by the time she reaches her third year.

They don't tell you that fresh skin can feel like chalk or what to do when it is hard to hold her hand because of it. They don't tell you what to do when the loving of someone is a hard, dark thing.

•

THE day my daughter is born, I watch the night darkness give way to dawn through contractions. Orange morning light spills past the cemetery to the east, but before she makes her way into the world, the light has gone out again. Somewhere overhead is a waxing crescent moon and in the distance the nightsounds of frogs waiting for rain.

She is born into the beauty of that night, screaming in the darkness as our bodies part for the first time.

•

ON the day they hang Peggy Facto in the Arsenal Lot, the March afternoon is warmed with the sun. The day is so uncharacteristically hot for these remote reaches of upstate New York, that by the time onlookers gather their belongings to begin the journey home, the ice has gone out on the lake. To return to Vermont, they are forced to wait their turn for the ferry to take their sleds and teams of horses across Lake Champlain, a cost they had not anticipated.

After the hanging, only Peggy's body is left, delivered to the Medical Society where young men gather around, jostling each other for a chance to glimpse her body laid out on a table. None of those crowding the table consider why it is only in death any of them note her presence or the cool white stretch of her arms.

•

"I didn't have help like you do," my mother says every time she holds my infant daughter. I have returned to the town of my own birth to care for my mother, but it is she who cares for my daughter and me. She watches my daughter while I take a shower, change my clothes, and find a space where there's blessed silence. A space where there are no demands on my body, no needs to fulfill other than my own. Here, I can pretend there's a world without my child. My mother calculates the minutes of this time that she gives. All this is a reckoning for her, all that she is giving me that she never got herself.

I allow her this small victory. I am alive after all.

•

A few roads away, a baby dies in the middle of the night.

•

It was dogs that found the body of Peggy Facto's baby late in the year of 1824. Just outside of town, the dogs careened through thickets of brambles and dense under-brush, their pointed snouts slanted forward to catch the scent. In the half-light of the woods, their furred bodies jostled against each other, the heat of their breath fogging the cool September air.

Caught on the scent of decay, the dogs pawed at the soft ground still not set by frost. Those dogs, how they would have rubbed first their heads and then their shoulders in the dirt before tilting over completely and wriggling in canine ecstasy. By the time men called off their burrowing dogs, the frost-heaved earth would have been rife with their prints and worked over under the weight of their bodies. But, through the debris on the ground, the refuse and rubbish from nearby houses, first one man and then the next caught sight of the small figure of the child. Tucked beneath scraps of forgotten metal and boards too weak to hold nails was a body wrapped in linen cloth. Inside the cloth lay a delicate collection of bones and skin scorched black, its sex inscrutable, yet the men could make out the wisps of fine hairs on its still soft skull.

•

On a September night in 2010, a baby cries, waking his parents. His nineteen year old mother brings him downstairs. She's the mother of twins which is, perhaps, why she brings her son down to the living room to give him a bottle. She leaves her daughter and partner upstairs to sleep while she changes his diaper and gives him a drink of water. I'd like to imagine her sitting with her son in these late hours, a small lamp casting them in gold as she holds him close on the couch and marvels at the movements of his fingers and flutter of his eyelids. I'd like to imagine this moment of maternal perfection instead of her bone-deep weariness and how angry it's possible for her to feel in those seconds of interruption. I'd like to imagine this because I know this is his end. She'll leave her son propped up on a chair as she returns to bed, but her six month old cannot maintain the position he's left in. Before morning, he'll be dead.

•

The dog barks through that night and morning, but still, the baby's parents sleep.

•

In my own September, my husband begins to sleepwalk. Our daughter is three months old and we've forgotten what it was to have dreamless nights of deep sleep. Instead, I dream of my own father's death, his body ravaged by cancer. In my dreams he dies and rises again, an endless resurrection. It is these dreams that wake me in the dark to find my bed empty.

Our baby is not crying when I find my husband on the upstairs landing, one arm curved in a U and the other gently moving in circles over empty air. I check our baby's crib, feeling and finding the heat of her body before I guide his sleepwalking body back to our bed. I spend hours every night keeping watch over them both, but I fight against my own body and its heavy pull back into sleep. Those nights are the nights my husband walks, holding a ghost child the same shape and size of our own.

•

Before the baby dies, Child Protective Services arrives at the couple's house one afternoon as part of an ongoing investigation. They knock, but there's no answer. Inside, the babies are crying and the dog begins to bark at the door. Investigators continue to knock while calling the mother's phone, but no one comes to the door or answers. By the time the State Police arrive on the scene more than twenty minutes has passed and everyone standing outside the home considers the situation an emergency. This is enough for them to break into the house. This is the sparse detail that we're given, that they break into the house, but I imagine them there with shoulders shoved against the door or knocking it out of its wood frame with sharp forceful kicks, something that would have sent a resounding crack through the house. I want the noise and the fury of flying debris, but there are probably other, gentler means to save babies in danger.

Once inside, the police and investigators find the babies unattended in the living room and as CPS workers attend to the children, the mother finally makes her way downstairs. I imagine her dressed in yoga pants and an oversized t-shirt, her long caramel hair caught up in a messy bun. Like this, she'd shuffle her feet across the carpet like a tired child, eyes still heavy. The investigators must have asked her questions, the contents of which I don't know. They record their warnings to her, though. That she should not leave her children unattended and certainly not alone on elevated or soft furniture. Your babies can suffocate like this, they say.

This is her own moment of reckoning, but she is alone in this space, answering these questions while upstairs her partner is still asleep.

•

PEGGY Facto marries a man who abandons her and their children. Later, everyone will gossip that her husband leaves her because she leads an unchaste lifestyle. Peggy doesn't respond. She is left on her own by the time she meets her lover, Francis Labare, a man who is married as well.

By the time Peggy Facto is pregnant with their child, no one speaks of her pregnancy. By August, her body is rounded, heavy with the baby taking shape inside of her. She had given birth before, but on the night her body prepares to deliver her lover's child, she begs him to bring her mother to her. Francis Labare ignores her request, ignores her pleas to bring Mrs. Chandreau, a midwife to the women in this desolate stretch of countryside. "I can do better than that old bitch," Francis Labare says.

Later, Peggy Facto will testify that she gave birth in her home with only Francis Labare there to assist her. That night, she says, he gathered their infant in his arms before he left her home. Peggy seems to say that her child was still alive when Francis Labare opened her front door, but we know little of this truth. Instead, imagine them there, all soaked with the blood of birthing. Imagine Peggy Facto finally alone in her dwelling, the remnants of childbirth strewn around her. Imagine the cold northern winds gathering outside. Imagine this, because when Francis Labare returns, he is alone.

•

ON the nights I hold my child feeding her from a bottle, I adjust my shirt, pulling it over my chest and to my neck so her skin won't touch my own. We both dislike this feeling of skin against skin despite what the doctors say about the necessity of bonding with your infant through touch and skin contact.

On these nights, we are restless together and we listen for the gray fox hunting in the woods behind our house. It kills other animals out there in the underbrush, just past the thorny brambles of the wild raspberry bushes. There's always a sharp guttural snarl and then silence as it too consumes its meal. Later, the fox will slip around the side of our house and down our driveway, but not before it calls out, its sharp voice like that of a woman screaming into the darkness.

•

During her trial, they say Peggy Facto took a string from her own dress and tied it around her child's neck before placing its body inside the hearth fire.

•

Peggy Facto's trial lasts less than half a day. She does not speak during the proceedings, but later she will be called to testify in the case against Francis Labare which occurs later that afternoon. The testimony during her own trial comes from locals who saw her pregnant with her child late in the month of August. The men who found the baby's body also take the stand and speak of their discovery.

During the sentencing, Judge Walworth suggests that this is not the first child that Peggy Facto murdered stating, "I am also constrained to say, it is much to be feared, that you will meet more than one murdered child, as an accusing spirit at the bar of Heaven."

Peggy Facto is ordered to be hung between the hours of twelve and two on the afternoon of March 18th after which her body will be delivered to the Medical Society for dissection. Francis Labare goes free.

•

I drive down the road where the baby and his sister lived with their parents before he died, my own child asleep in her car seat, only the movement of my vehicle keeping her in that state. It's a long stretch of road, beginning at the Canadian border and ending 325 miles away in Laurel, Delaware. But here, in the county where it begins, this piece of asphalt feels like our own as it passes by farm fields and houses that sag low towards the ground. There are roadside markers for battles and important occasions, but there are none noting the place this child spent his life. I pass each residence wondering if this was the place he was last.

It was his father who woke in the morning to find him in the chair where his mother left him the night before. The baby's heart had long stopped beating, his body gone cold.

•

As they bring Peggy Facto to the hanging, the band plays a jaunty melody, "Soldier's Joy," to accompany the procession of people to the Arsenal Lot. Local citizens have appealed to Governor DeWitt Clinton for clemency, but he denies their requests.

Instead, the execution progresses on schedule. Before the band picks up, Peggy Facto is taken from her prison cell, her body weak with the confinement. Several men support her until she is brought to the wagon that takes her to the gallows.

The procession is led by Captain Sailly, one of the men who petitioned for her release. He leads the local Light Infantry and another local man leads the Rifle Company. Women, young and old, form the end of this death parade. At the gallows, a prayer is said before Peggy Facto declares her innocence. It does not matter, they drop the noose around her neck and set the bolt free.

Peggy Facto dies quickly.

•

In the early months of her life, I set my daughter on the floor. I want to say that I get down with her and stare up at the ceiling, the surface covered with popcorn spackling and so much gold glitter it looks like the night sky. I want to say we look for constellations and I tell her of Orion the Hunter, the only constellation that has ever made me feel centered and safe.

Instead, I place her on the floor. Clench my hands into fists so hard that moon-shaped indents redden my palms. Every night we wait for my husband to get done with work, and each minute that passes that he doesn't return makes my heart feel like it's stuttering in my chest.

•

By the time she is twenty-one, the mother of the six month old infant will leave a courtroom sobbing. The District Attorney releases a statement after she is sentenced to one to three years in prison for criminally negligent homicide. The DA writes, "[His] death was absolutely preventable. Hopefully, this case will be a reminder of how precious our children are and what an immense responsibility it is to have their lives in our hands."

•

BEFORE she is even six months old, my daughter begins to cry when I go to her room to care for her in the night instead of her father. "She's a daddy's girl," everyone we encounter will say to me as a piece of consolation. It feels more like a judgement.

When she finally begins to speak, my daughter will start screaming "No!" instead. And, by the time she gathers more words, she starts to sing out instead of crying, "Daddy, come back! I miss you!" Her tiny voice carries all the way down the stairs from her bedroom to the living room. She never calls for me. When she was born we'd alternate these nighttime needs, each taking turns with our child but, I stop going, tired of both of our tears.

"There will come a time when she'll only want you," my mother will say. She's desperate for signs of my connection to my daughter, calling attention to even the smallest gestures. "See!" she'll declare every time my daughter holds my hand.

I begin to wonder less about these moments and more about the limits of my daughter's forgiveness. How much is it that I can ask of her.

•

MY daughter's name means lively or to live.

PIMONE TRIPLETT

Recital for Mixed-Race Player

       Off key, off color,
disguised as clavichord in cardboard,
       split
level, fretting over something
       forgotten. Beholden
to majors and minors, latter of whom
       could least afford
losing members. Daily followed
       the iron-railed flights,
fancies, leading up, leading down,
       with sponsors, frazzled,
doing their best with the mess. Also, made
       sparkling repertoires
of much affection, bought
       the bridge-pins in bulk
for dampening effects.

       One afternoon an alleged-
to-be-larger audience arrived, took its place
       in the basement. Other
children, women, fellow players, all. At first,
       faces rose underlit,
so lovely, the hushed hailing of pedaled
       action, song
swooning, randy with make-believe
       and erasure. I imagined
they heard the same.
       Mistakes occurred.
Then a mild legato in the tune
       crashed into the *what*

are you's of *rattatat* and *reach*. Fumbled for
            the single chord
expected. Weights above, pressings of pad.
            Soon bone and knuckle
whole notes, tenderly or in rush,
            became a timbre uncovering
stolen ivory keys taken from a beast.
            Stay back.
Stay confusion, I thought, sinking
            inside pound
and pianoforte, the heard, some treble
            and bass
that, muddling, made us.

SASHA WEST

[those were the days of]

I don't know   I don't know

antibiotics spread   ozone depletion spreads

I wanted to be the painter

on a New York roof   coming into

her own   mid-forties

I didn't know

what we were   looking for

my most prized possession

was a child

I couldn't   possess

her at all   sometimes

she came close to me

like an animal   in a pasture wandering up

to the fence   I adored her most

when her hand patted   my breast

as if to say

      alright   alright

she narrowed the possibilities

as did   the man in my bed

to only   our happiness

which I had begged for   from the world

so often   and with such longing

ALEX CHERTOK

Picking Apples at 30

One foot on the ladder under the dangling Galas.
The tree sags with its bumper crop. Apples
dragging on the grass like old wrinkly knuckles.
The fruit he holds is overripe. His thumb dents it.
This one by his head has a white pate of spider webs.
This one's been too long in the sun, one half burned,
venous-bloody, crow's-footed, the other half
pale as a child kept too long in a cellar. It all falls
silent when he lets the one with the lump drop.
He remembers now. He's waited too long. Who knows
what's grown down there. What bitter pit, what
fire blight. What scabs and bug-bitten swellings.
He should know better. What flyspeck and sooty blotch,
what blemish. In the shower he'll check, hunched
like a man fumbling over an overhand knot.
He rolls each one gently between his fingers,
picking spurs off stems. Each tip stings. He's not
orchard-strong. He knows no knots. No cures.
How close he feels to the tree's heartwood from in here.
This one wears a coat of wax to keep itself alive.
How to steel himself against what can't be staved off.
What knows no softness. Such a small thing. But too big
to grasp. In the shower he'll let out a breath
from deep in his own dark pith, bracing himself.

KEVIN CRAFT

Among the Cypresses (23 Remedies)

Cut them down
or plant them in long rows tiger-
striping a country lane, still they harbor
hangnail shades, sighs of the dead: so were said

to shoot up suddenly in the harshest soils,
unsolicited, like any bird sprung
from their useless fruit. Mourning tree,
says Pliny: dowry for a daughter. Make me

a poultice of leaves for the snakebite
riding my ankle like an angry tattoo.
For you who've gone missing
in the vertical shadow,

who knock hardhearted in the deadbolt trunk—
salvo or echo, some bystander rage: sing me
the password to your dumbstruck grief.
Ring true. For every year hollowed out

of blind disbelief
another swings on its axis like high noon's curfew—
an epoch of abscess,
self-immolation.

If we could take Pliny at his word,
follow the sweep
of Spartan shadow, trace hernia
and sunstroke to their forgone source . . .

But nothing comes of it
but miscalculation, nothing but axle-grease
and bean meal for the swelling of the testes,
laughter the keenest of medicinal gulls.

Yet here they linger by the harbor,
these cypresses, pressing whose lost
sailor cause? Watch them ravage a hillside
in Languedoc, bear the writ of mistral

whiplash, scour the sky of its least adieu.
To be topmast and sarcophagus both—
to guard every graveyard
with monastic glee: is that harm's way,

or no harm done? It's the slow motion
sickness gets you in the end—you born out of
a thousand narrow escapes, breath
too close to call. Spare me

the tapering apex, spare me the generous
wick, dear witness, green as a god
or a lie. What I wouldn't give—a long arm,
a longer leg—
                    to eat the wind out of goodbye.

ZEINA HASHEM BECK

And Still, the Sun

after Pablo Neruda's "Walking Around"

I happen to be tired of being

> an Arab. My worst, my best childhood memory is listening
> to the news every morning, in my dad's car. I waited
> for the tunnel—the interrupted signal, the mountain silence.

The smell of barbershops makes me wail.

> I skip the headlines about the CIA tortures, the elections, the war—
> the newspaper words crawl up my arms like black ants. I read about
> Mercury, how it might help me speak, how Venus might orbit love my way.

I happen to be tired of my feet and my nails

> and *zaatar*, and olive oil, and the scent of bread from the bakery downstairs.
> The siren outside weeps into my window, the distance. The coffee
> rises in the kettle, the cigarette smoke burns my eye.

Nevertheless it would be delightful

> to believe all those things my *teita* said about *Amerka*—
> everyone there is civilized, and free. And they have street
> numbers, and they know how to queue when they're supposed to.

I don't want to go on being a root in the dark.

> A black friend once told me, "Black is like
> Third-World, you know, like Arab."
> (how we carry names and meanings)

I don't want for myself so many misfortunes—

    the way Mezzeh will always mean Syrian prison,
    will invoke that TV image of a man with blue swollen legs.
    My mother said he was among the lucky ones. I was ten.

This is why Monday burns like petroleum—

    for what else burns here?
    Houses, and childhood, and olive trees. And still,
    the sun, and all this laughter and singing.

And it pushes me into certain corners, into certain moist houses—

    My friend who grew up in Syria says Mezzeh
    has beautiful cactus trees, says she first kissed there,
    first smoked, talks her way into the heart of Damascus.

There are brimstone-colored birds and horrible intestines

    and cyclamens on the mountains of my childhood—
    pink and fragrant like newborn babies
    among the rocks. Here, open mouths. Here, leaf hearts.

I walk around with calm, with eyes, with shoes,

    although the sound of a washing machine
    in the middle of the night made me scream, shake, ask
    if we had a gun in the house, if we knew how to use it.

Notes:

Each one-line stanza is the first line (or part of the first line) of each stanza of Pablo Neruda's "Walking Around."

Teita is Arabic for "grandmother."

DAN BEACHY-QUICK

from A Quiet Book (47, 49, 50, 51)

47.

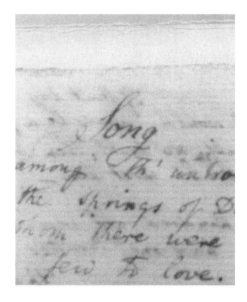

WRITTEN IN WILLIAM WORDSWORTH'S HAND, photographed from the correspondence with Briggs and Cottle, a Song from the *Lyrical Ballads*, found among many poems in manuscript, including the "Preface" in the author's own hand. Among the poems, written on paper as large as a poster, one crossed out, and written in darker ink above: "N.B. do not print the following poem. W. W." The poem begins at the lower margin of a page, continuing atop the next column, crossed out with a large X.

•

·

Song
a pastoral

Fly, written
day   of
stoves
this
Arms

your languages
song   kettle
poker   of
away   fury
plate   metal

```
earth                made
pulses             slower
     in              was
  heaven      knows
       is     degrees


      a disconsolate
           field or
             him!
          poor fool
          the   edge


          fumbles
         completely
             out
             and
            brink


           stands
           he has
        methinks   can
          West    the
          neither    first


     sink       him
  heaving       lost
   death        blood
  pretty        blue
                   frost


 companion,       while
    from          cheek
  glad            desolate
 summer              floor
  were


witness                  helpless
                          thing
```

<pre>
              comes

                                      crowds
                                      sound
        the   clouds
</pre>

•

To my eye, the words crossed out begin to form the helix of life's most buried struc-
ture, but it's only the shape of the lines that mark out what exists as no longer existing.

I think of the poem as a kind of pastoral in reverse. Or do I mean the underneath
of the field.

I know the poem isn't very good. It's not meant to be.

•

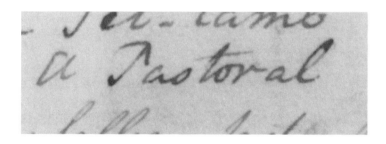

•

I took many photos of lines Wordsworth crossed out, but he did so with such thor-
oughness, that no words could be read underneath their own negation—but I know
they're there.

(Somewhere, I hear a whisper as if whispering to itself about the passion of presence
in absence, or is the passion of absence in presence.)

•

Nota Bene:

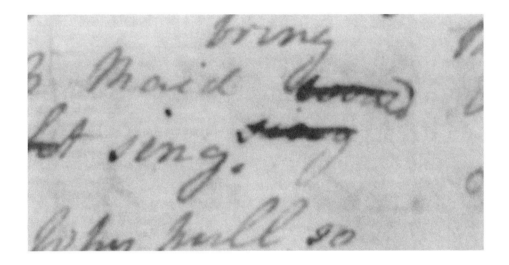

•

I hear both words sing. I think I do. I think both words are still singing. Maybe to each other in the dark of the closed box where they live. Maybe to you and me. Maybe to a box called time, which is kept in the library in a different room.

49.

IN THE TEMPORARY READING ROOM of the rare book library a man in stained glasses has three faces at once. He stares out into the room where the readers read, and on either side of his face, his profile. I couldn't see behind him, even though he's made of glass, so I can't be sure, but feel safe assuming, that the eyes looking forward stare also behind. It's hard to tell if he's some kind of monster or god, or just a man looking from side to side where passing time is caught in a single, simultaneous instant because the motion can be caught in no other way; or if, as I fear is true, his visage is demonstration to each of us sitting within the room he gazes into of the consequences of reading: another face comes into your face, and who you are is no longer your own.

I went to the library to look for what is lost, but everything in the library has been found. I hoped, in some haphazard way, to look for lines crossed out, language discarded after being called up from the mind as not right or not worthy, orphan words, or are they exiles, to gather them in these pages, and give them a home.

A séance of a kind, to ask the librarian for a name and she walks behind a door and returns carrying the voice of the dead in a box.

Every April over the course of many years Thoreau kept track of the weather. In brown ink he scrawled the observations so quickly the words outpaced the letters forming them.

April weather alternate rain [   ] 30 -53

              quite   rain   Ap 2-52
              nest   walking
rain rain   Ap 15-52

(Easter   17)—wind heaves [?] water in the rain

april flowers 13 -53

April 1st—54 raining steady april day
April rain

heavy thunder shower
        3 days of rain precipitation

        noon finds rather warm rain
    a misting rain the night after

I like it when the cloud fills the mind to remind it that the cloud repeats in the mind like a rhyme that never perfectly rhymes. The mist in the night obscures darkness already obscure, and to know it exists, you must walk through it.

Thoreau's sister Sophia gave to an orphanage for colored children a handwritten copy of the end of *Walden*, but it isn't the ending the rest of us know.

I do not say that John
or Jonathan—that this gen-
eration or the next, age
[   ] this [   ] or the next
will realize all this—but
such is the character of that
morrow which mere lapse
of time can never make to
dawn.
    The light which puts out our
eyes is darkness to us. There is a
dawn lurking behind the hills of
every horizon at noontide[?]; there are ears that
hear the drowsy crickets, and eyes that see the glistening
dews even then. Only that day dawns to which we
are awake. There is more day to dawn; the sun is but
a morning star.

A word might be considered a "colored child"; there's no other way to see them. A white child disappears into the blankness. Against the margin of the page, Thoreau as he neared its end, had to write smaller and smaller to fit all the words in. I guess in the end he felt the extra sentence made a mob, and sent them out, to make a life of their own, drinking the dew for water, soothed by the music of the cricket's song.

But for Thoreau the outside was an inside, the head a tool for burrowing, and the man who measured the cellar of the new Concord Court House—

    To whom it may
        concern.

    [other side]

    Concord Mass
        Aug. 15th 1850

    This may certify
    that I have this day
    measured the sand
    excavated for the cellar
    of the new Court
    House in this town, and
    found it to be six-
    hundred and six and
    a half—606½ cubic
    yards.

                Henry D. Thoreau
                        Surveyor.

—the land of deepest exile, of furthest wandering, had for horizon a line within. On a page torn from a notebook and found in another book bound this letter he wrote to no one, or one, or you—

    discovery of America [   ]
    of the adventures of the faithful explain
    [   ]own interior. Here is the center of
    Central Africa—I would say then any
    vagrant countrymen [   ]
    foreign theater for spectacles—consider
    first that there's nothing which can
    delight or astonish the eye—but you may
    discover it all in yourselves. [   ]
    thoughtlessly after the setting sun for ad-
    ventures, for there [   ] the beast you

have imagined. If you would be a
soldier here is demanded the eye and the
nerve. What after all is the meaning
of that exploring expedition with all its
parade and expense—but just a recog-
nition after fact that there are continents
and seas in the moral world which
[   ] all
unexplained by him [
                                    ] thousand miles through
cold and storm, savage cannibals and savage
[   ] home and reflect—easier
to flee before one's life than face it.
We are all defeated [?] –this is the reason
we enlist. Know thyself is the motto of
the true explorer. The man heedlessly
obeys the first blind impulse, and hastens
to South Africa perchance to chase the

other side of page

giraffe, but that is not the game he would
be after. How long pray would he hunt giraffes
if he could?—As soon as one brave
sailor shall declare that he has fathomed
the deeps of life and found them shallow
then may he enlist for the first Guinea
voyage [   ] offer.—Let a [ ]
man face all the fools of existence, and
he will be ready for any service that may
offer elsewhere. For the [   ]
those that go blindly into trade and
cease to think, those cowards that
[   ] away and enlist, have been daunted
from the [   ] of the field—they could
not stand alone with their lives—Men
whom I meet in the street are so
[   ] outward bound—they live out
[   ]—they are going and coming—looking
before and behind them—all out of [   ]

in 'the air'. I would fain see
them inward bound setting in and in
further every day. When I inquired I
should [   ] that one had gone away—
where, [

          ] he had entered deeper within
the folds of being.
[   ] who could speak all tongues
[

                                        ]

Relics, too, in boxes. Small prayers to presence that make absence so real it's felt on
the nerves.

This hand-hewn pine beam, probably part of a stud or rafter is from Thoreau's
cabin at Walden Pond, and was hewed himself as described on pp. 66-69 of
'Walden', with the bark, as there noted, left on one side. The nails, also from the
cabin, are presumably those described on pp. 69-71 of 'Walden', taken from the
shanty he bought from James Collins for $4.25.

These nails that held the cabin at Walden Pond together were taken from it when the cabin was pulled apart. I like how the nails speak of the wholeness within which a life lives itself, how it is built by piercing into what's holy or whole.

The force that bent the nail came from Thoreau's own arm, so different from reading in a book a word he wrote, or in his own hand the same, to feel the muscle swing the tool, hammer still somehow in the air, and the three-faced man in the glass looking everywhere to see from which direction the blow will come.

Except the blow comes from within.

The librarian takes from me what I have borrowed, all of it borrowed, what I've borrowed, all of it. Thoreau had to return what he had borrowed, too:

Dear Sir,

I return to the library Marquette's "Recit des Voyage" in the unbound reprint and volume.

Sign respectfully,
Henry D. Thoreau

50.

The muses are daughters of memory
Clio, Terpsichore

But the poet only mentions the muse of History, and the muse of the Delight of Dance, as if the others have been, or need to be, forgotten.

Beauty is difficult

Helios

Hard to know if the poet's stating back to the god what the god already knows. But I guess beauty isn't difficult for a god, whose shining out of himself is his own shining source, but for the one who must say "Helios," all who are not Helios, beauty is difficult. Hard to know if Helios is the example of difficult beauty. Hard to know if it's a prayer, an affirmation, a plea for release.

•

The poems Ezra Pound wrote in the prisoner of war camp at Pisa are written in pencil on two different kinds of paper. The majority of the poems appear on the ruled notebook paper a child in grade school practices her alphabet on, blue lines across the gray page, like wires made out of sky on an overcast day. He would turn the page sideways so the lines ran up and down, and in two columns, one left, one right, he'd write his Cantos. The words paced behind the blue bars like an animal in a cage, prisoners too, or so it felt to me, holding the pages in the reading room, while the man in stained glass above me looked in every direction at once, as if looking everywhere for something that had gone missing, or worrying from which direction the threat will come.

Pound seldom crosses out a single word, and checking the lines against the published poems, all that changes are the lengths of the lines, as if—let out from the cage in which they were composed—they could walk further toward the margin before turning around.

He writes in ancient Greek:

ΟΥ ΤΙΣ	{"noman" as Odysseus gave his name to Polyphemus
δειλια δεινα	{"cowardice of whom one cannot or will not name"
ποικιλοθεον αθανατα	{deathless many-colored bird
μεταθομενον! . . .	{appeasing by sacrifice
Κυθερα! Κυθερα!	{Cytherea, Cytherea, one among Aphrodite's many names
εθος	{ethos

I could link them into their own poem, if only to interpret it:

I am the one I am not,
unable to say what I am afraid of though I know I am
afraid, of what I cannot name, and the soul
best described as a bird of shifting colors
has offered herself to the goddess of Desire
so that she might be appeased and let me live,
noman that I am, a virtuous life.

But mostly I'm making this up.

The other paper, given him by Lt. White whose name Pound underlines thrice, is a pamphlet of airmail stationary, 80 blank pages meant to "save money on your postage." Within those 80 pages, loose because the weak glue has eroded away, is the poem I came to the library to see, Canto LXXXI, whose lines *What thou lovest well remains / the rest is dross / What thou lov'st well shall not be reft from thee / what thou lov'st well is thy true heritage* have etched themselves with a silent chisel into my head or heart.

Love is difficult
Cytherea

Page after page, as on the blue-lined notebook paper, the pencil's pressure pushing down through the thin sheet and leaving the impression on the next page of the words written before, flow from the poet so fluidly it seems a god must be speaking them in his ear. But then, when he gets to the passage that—almost every semester—I read out loud to my students, he falters, crosses out, rewrites, changes and reverts, as if the god stopped speaking, or began speaking in more than one voice, and each voice spoke at once:

> "~~Thine eyes two will slaye me~~
> ~~sodenly,~~
> ~~I may the beautie of them~~
> ~~not sustayne."~~
> ~~from airy sound, not~~
> ~~worked so patiently,~~
> ~~my sprite no turned not~~
> ~~to me agayne~~
> ~~Till I had heard the father~~
> ~~of all rhyme~~
> ~~speak time's ingle~~
> ~~where he~~ [   ] ~~me~~

They return, the old ones:

> As I was listening to the
> enchanted song
> There came new
> subtlety of eyes
> within my tent
> whether of spirit or hypostasis
> w/ glad hilarities
> came no entire face
> but what the blindfold hides,
> ~~of every~~
> or at carnival
> nor any pair showed
> anger
> but as unaware
> of other presence
> smiled, each pair as at
> loveliest
> nor was there space not
> a full <u>eidos</u>

but if how every soul lives is by
                    own
+ proper space, + each of
                    these
can penetrate + interpass
        as light through light
casting but shade before no
        other lights
nor lose its forms, each soul
        keeping its cosmos
interlaid/laced free passing

They return, the old ones:

                    nor any pair
showed of anger
        ~~it was not the sole~~
        at others presence
~~but seemed~~
    as careless or unaware
as it had the not the
                    whole
tent's space
~~as these were masks not~~
                    ~~masks~~
~~but had their loveliest life~~
        ~~six pair~~
~~nor was not all~~
                    ~~but certainty~~
        sky's clear
        night's sea
        green of the mountain pool
~~shone from the masks~~
                    ~~not masks~~
shone from the unmasked
        eye,
in half-mask's room.
what thou lovest well
        shall not be rent from thee
what thou lovest well, remains

     the rest is dross
what thou lovest well is thy
     true heritage
whose world, or [   ] or
       thing
or _____ is it of none
so, thinking [?] of althea [?] at the [   ]
two rose like lips pressed down
     upon my own

They return, the old ones:

   first comes the seen
   then thus the palpable
   ~~[   ] to make Elysium~~
     ~~with~~
   ~~dost thou lived in hell~~

              ~~as twere~~
              ~~in halls~~
              ~~of hell~~

     ~~mined~~
     ~~jailed~~
   Elysium, ~~penetrant~~
   ~~e'en [   ]~~
   ~~dominant laughing~~
   ~~at bay of hell chill~~
   ~~making game of hell~~
   ~~even of hell~~
   ~~making her sport even~~
          ~~of hell~~

Hell is a place where repetition reigns, keeps crossing itself out to make itself seen, where what is is by no longer existing, a pitkin ploughed through verse to pour in seed or blood or anything to appease the dead or placate the gods, a kind of vision or revision that never alters the mistake, but makes it over again.

Of heaven, I know considerably less.

But I did learn a new prayer, a small one:

O lynx guard my
              vineyard
as the grape swells
      under vines

It's not in any liturgy, just written behind blue lines. It's a strange prayer because it is so true. Protect the grape from the sun that ripens it. Beauty is difficult, Helios. We must learn to grow a leaf that shades us from our source, or the source will end us. Δειλια δεινα. How to tell the difference between terror and wonder, I don't know; the word says they are the same. Μεταθομενον! O lynx that laps that raisins off the vines.

51.

Sir Thomas Browne writes:

. . . wee doe but learne today, what our better advanced judgements will unteach us to morrow: and *Aristotle* doth but instruct us as *Plato* did him; that is, to confute himselfe. I have runne through all sorts, yet finde no rest in any; though our first studies and & *junior* endeavors may stile us Peripateticks, Stoicks, or Academicks, yet I perceive the wisest heads prove at last, almost all Skepticks, and stand like *Janus* in the field of knowledge. I have therefore one common and authentick Philosophy I learned in the Schooles, whereby I discourse and satisfy the reason of other men; another more reserved and drawne from experience whereby I content my owne. *Solomon* that complained of ignorance in the height of knowledge, hath not onely humbled my conceits, but discouraged my endeavors. There is yet another conceit that hath sometimes made me shut my books; which tels mee it is a vanity to waste our dayes in the blind pursuit of knowledge; it is but attending a little longer, and wee shall enjoy that by instinct and infusion which we endeavor at here by labour and inquisition: it is better sit downe in a modest ignorance, & rest contented with the natural blessings of our owne reasons, then by the uncertaine knowledge of this life, with sweat and vexation, which death gives every foole gratis, and is an accessory of our glorification."

These lessons learned best in the Library: to close the book, to look up and look around, the far horizon isn't knowledge or wisdom, but the distance from which wild ignorance daily bounds. From all sides that limit rides silently toward us; fate gallops on invisible horses. We wake and find the horizon has fit itself to the profile of our own face; we wake to find our face is made mostly of distance. All those miles fate had ridden across it also gathered and compressed, formed for us into a kind of mask we never asked to wear, and not knowing if already it's on us, know not how to take it off; so it is one keeps waiting for one's own face to arrive, limit of the farthest extent grown so strangely intimate, making what is most my own most mysterious, as if the world's whole distance had made itself at home in a visage. Fate promises there is a world we live in of which we know hardly a thing, and the nearer it comes, the less we understand it. Studying doesn't help much, but still one reads the books, heads like grain-heavy wheat bent down. The days pass, and each day we look around unceasingly in all directions; we even look out the back of our heads. From which directions is our ignorance coming? Looking up from our books, what is the expression in the mouth, of the eyes? Apprehension. Cross-listed, in the Library, with Hope, with Fear, subsets of the larger worry, Understanding.

Translation Folio

TATIANA SHCHERBINA

Translator's Introduction

J. Kates

THE LITERARY GENERATION IN WHICH Tatiana Shcherbina reached maturity is one of particular ambiguity. Born in 1954, the year after the death of Stalin, she graduated from the Moscow State University with a degree in French literature and a thesis in classical studies during an era of official caution, if not outright repression. Of the "generation of the 1960s" that immediately preceded her own, Shcherbina said, "Their poetry lived on platforms, and they addressed the millions. . . . The new generation must bring new ideas, new attitudes of poetry." Her own cohort took as their models the relatively quiet voices of "Akhmatova's orphans" (of whom the exemplar was Brodsky in exile) and the avant-garde poets from earlier in the twentieth century. Shcherbina said in a 1990 interview, "Poetry should return to the tradition that existed before the sixties generation. The new generation must bring new ideas, new attitudes to poetry." These two statements she regarded not as contradictory, but complementary.

During the late 1980s, Shcherbina emerged as a popular spokesperson for a growing independent cultural movement that blossomed under the clearing skies of perestroika. By schooling and temperament—educated in the Greek classics and drawn by affinity to French culture—Shcherbina looked abroad; and in fact, during the first half of the 1990s (at a time when Anatoly Naiman said, "All [Russian] compasses point west") she lived in Paris and worked with Radio Liberty in Munich. She has long since returned to Moscow, where she has established her career as a cultural commentator, a prose-writer, an editor and—of course—as a poet.

Shcherbina was the first contemporary poet I met when I traveled to Moscow in 1986, and she was the first I worked at translating, attracted as I was to her challenging word-play. I had grown up during the Cold War, when wit, verbal pyrotechnics and light humor were not qualities I had associated with "Soviet" literature. I could not have imagined a Russian poet writing scurrilous limericks about her forebears:

> Pasternak, like us all, was born nude.
> He pewked and he puled and he mewed
> Till he swapped in his nappy
> For something more snappy
> And a sex life especially crude.

or these lines from the very first poem of hers I translated:

> Snap—Boom—Zing:
> my mother's a sun descended from yellow melons,
> father a boomerang of moons a lunar elk,
> between them a euclidean parallel:
> *il* mirroring *il*, *elle* mirroring *elle*.

In her more recent work in the landscape of a tumultuous and evermore uncertain Russian scene, Shcherbina has become if anything more explicit, more political, and less reliant on linguistic gymnastics for their own sake. She might be seen as returning to some of the ideas and attitudes of the poets of the 1960s, but carrying over the lightness of her previous writing. She has embraced the technological innovations of the twenty-first century with both the glee of a bureaucrat celebrating the "electrification of the whole country" and the contrary cynicism of a worldly-wise historian recognizing too many of their implications and limitations. As ever, she is reflective, contradictory, and, as I put it nearly two decades ago, writing with a vatic voice speaking not of what is to come, but of what is.

(This commentary has been in part excerpted and condensed from my foreword to *The Score of the Game* [Zephyr Press, 2003], including Shcherbina's full book *Null Null* and a selection of other poems.)

TATIANA SHCHERBINA : Four Poems

The Airplane

Lightning struck the airplane
and the Muse abandoned me.
Loneliness began chirping
more insistently, like a jellyfish
revolving its translucent body
and my plane turns
around, in vain
I am looking for a sandbank.

The airplane breaks through
a swelling cloud to a point of return,
everything in it is brittle:
from the simple electric discharge
it rolls downward
as if stung, and me with it.
Our life is gravitation,
it drags us down.

But it was only a fainting fit,
and landed skillfully
as flat as a ham.
The Muse, who lived not far away,
and I were both lucky
in the night and the gentle weather.
The plane was a crisis
manager. Or something like that.

April 2005
London

Intimate Relations

I connect with God the way
I'd like the computer
to hook up with me.
Yea, I cling to it and it glitches me pink.
Each *delete* is a heart-rending cry
of a universally catatastrophic
"What for!" Existed—
until I chucked the files into the trash,
not for what, but not for nothing.
The Trojans move away on automatic
without any discussion.

Somehow the gift horse which
(as we say in Russian) you shouldn't look in the teeth,
downloaded a sweet valentine
and ate into my memory. "eat incubi!"—
I call, called out: "idiot."
The user does not notice the pernicious netski,
An archangel with wings keeps vigil—a postman.
The devil spattered with bald patches knocks on the floor:
"You've won a million."
The world, blocked up not childishly
deinstalls itself like a dream.

With each new processor
I obey all the faster,
I do not pose personal questions,
and the computer
as it were finds my groove:
I say *insert*, and this means, "ease it on in,"
I say: change to a roman font,
and this means, *alt shift*—but it doesn't like this,
it groans, doesn't understand, what's this,
but it's no longer talking to me:
shove your antivirus up your own ass.

Gagarin

The USSR had Gagarin
until the superman crashed
and the superpower crashed,
on the dream of a peaceful private life.
Gagarin, the first to leap off Earth,
but who then knew there is nowhere to run.
Nowhere to run: everywhere hot spots,
burning stars, icy planets,
The cosmos too is a shambles of stones.
By default, a world of optical illusions.
Gagarin did not meet God in orbit,
So he told us, no god, but he hoped, meaning, there is—
The notion that we evolved from bacteria
self-procreated by chance in a Universe
of science fiction utopia
gave way to euphoria.
Space seemed so foreign God was resurrected
and superman interred.
A pioneer of Space hammered the last nail
into that long romantic history,
for which so many now
would give their sober minds.

London has raised a statue to Gagarin,
and a question: what face now for Russia,
Russia, with faces by the trunkful?
Tolstoy's? To everyone a Shakespeare
and their own one-eyed war hero
and other harbingers of degradation,
but only one man popped the cork off Earth
and humankind became smaller and smaller,
almost bacteria
because seeing themselves from space
they cannot be otherwise.

The Second Coming

All that's needed is a second coming.
What the first was worth is easy to reckon up:
Each of us gave birth to a new "we,"
but now we have sufficiently fed, shod and clad one another
no new clamps, new lands or new recipes.
The dead languages of religion no longer help;
we have been turned into rumbling volcanoes,
tectonic faults, hoofbeats, into *ko-te.*
Gentle tigers, cheeky monkeys,
hippopotami saving their baby hippos,
stray dogs—that's us, and we cry mercy.

But, this is no longer "we," it's a whim: we are wee mice.
We are weekend serials, we are whoa and we are whee, where we is not I.
From time to time we connected to a network—recharging
hurts—shocking—but what's next?
We killed, warning, "Keep out—fatal!"
but when the batteries of the world order hook up
a horrible end looks better than than endless horror.

Water pumped out with care, something in me come to an end,
I'm all for drilling and filling, but without the stamina,
connection broken, a discord, the DNS server doesn't answer.
Energy builds an altar and requires a sacrifice.
It is written: Keep out—fatal!, but thirst is a torment.
Care is not needed here, only decision.
(The fifth cup of coffee, the tenth cigarette,
the twelfth year in the trenches, minus twenty.
On Crete, on Corfu? *Away-from-Moscow* I watch for a carriage,
I do not fly, but my thinking: to-fly-or-stay.)

The Earth is an urban village,
everyone knows one other, at least as a Like on facebook,
and in the Amazon rainforest not quetzalcoatls
are hiding, but only those only in the extreme design
failed by the stakes of the "exotic,"

Thanks to those scouts Fraser and Levi-Strauss.
One billion could have taken it all, that's done.
Two billion could have spoken it all, that's spoken.
And who could have guessed how civilization looks,
we are archival rats, wireless mice,
videocameras, paparazzi,
he has not yet come, the one who lives on the roof,
here—fall in love, breathing in breathing out, and fall.

Translated from the Russian by J. Kates

ED BOK LEE

Gwangju, South Korea

They were lost   In a country where everything seems green cab
and the only water—dream-tongue   slow and oceanic spittle
The father's face interrogated   into a street sign
The mother's way   with plants all feasted upon by soldiers
ganged into rusted thought-trains   The sister was
there, but selling faceless clocks   an aquarium on a corner
Everyone else was a cousin   never met
You were there too   a bayonet   asking directions for

for hair   So you forced,   Everywhere—Natives with hot black sails

                    peeled away a face

to reveal the sky's cords   All more vocal than your own

None reasonable, nor lovely enough to swallow   And once again, you were mistaken
answering the wrong question

But the horse-faced street walker wouldn't let go   What you remember now:
Her smoky, torn voice   her bandaged hand guiding
past children cheering a helicopter's military loud-   a story of a nearby shack on a mountain
speaker
                    farmed into a grain of sand

Nothing of the hills' burnt-down Buddhist temples   the looted tombs at the hem of town or
     tattoo on her sun-scored cheekbone

The land's yellow loess whispered   *You could go deeper*
and   *Beware the rutting*
American dump trucks—small and distant   enough to churn any old thought
song
     I take you each evening to the clouds,
     howled her old man, hobbling
to introduce us—
     This, a languid traveler's further logic:

Maybe he was instead a god   and she loved him
in   another time before
all the skyscrapers, karaoke bars, banks,   U.S. Army red-light camptowns

If you saw us, both of them cajoling,   tugging each one of my sleeves,
you too may have hoped for   a disgorgement of silver and
     peonies—

In whichever lifetime,   At whichever dusk

     your own tide bleeds

ELEANOR MARY BOUDREAU

[Wedding Planning]

I begin to dread the surf and turf. I cross
then double cross another friend off of the list. Now this,
"The jaws of leopard seals and grizzly bears are similar,
except the leopard seals' are twice as big. They're also more intelligent."
God knows my mother likes to tell me things
I do not want to know in restaurants.
"This scientist, she studied icebergs in Antarctica.
She watched them drift and scour the sea floor,
and the ensuant loss of life and habitat—"
This story I know cold and could deglove.

Snow settled round the research base, like a halo.
The ancient face, the surface, of the bay
under a layer of jostling, floating crags—"brash ice."

Birds flew in fists into the teeth of sky.
Whether she believed in god or anything below us,
wind furred the shallows and she snorkeled out.

"The leopard seal attacked from underneath
and so she must have seen the open jaws, the teeth. She screamed,
was dragged, her dive computer says, to a depth of 230 feet."

Just as revenge, a dish, is best served cold,
I cross another friend off of my list.
A punishment should be immediate,
but accident cannot be reckoned with.
This is the myth inside decorum—
and what I've ordered never does arrive.

[Pantoum: What You Are Eating as Metaphor for What You Want Right Now]

You turn the brownie into two brownies
by cutting it in two.
You didn't think a boy could break your daughter's heart, especially not that one,
but there it is.

By cutting it in two
he broke your daughter's heart.
There it is—in two pieces.
She thinks of me as she looks at the ocean.

"He broke my heart, Mom."
Do you ever get bored of hearing it?
"We were sitting on a park bench, looking out at the water and we thought of you."
—Crying an ocean—

Do you ever get bored of hearing it? The crickets in the park
make their cricket sounds
—crying an ocean—you know what crickets sound like. They sound nice
their entire bodies vibrating.

The crickets make their cricket sounds.
You hear through the phone the one sound you never wanted to hear—and it is creaking.
You know what crickets sound like—nice.
I look down as the green slats run through my thighs.

The one sound you never wanted to hear—and it's breaking.
You cut the brownie in two.
I stare down at the green running through my thighs.
I didn't think a boy could break my heart, but there it is—

two pieces.

ALEXANDRA HAINES-STILES

The Salvages

after T. S. Eliot

I don't know much about gods, but I think
they must live inside copper and glass and silicon
just as they do in the roiling waves, the tides, the moon,
in the ascension of heavy steel tubes traversing the Atlantic,
fearful views from on high fueled by their magic.
In the mystic haze steaming off phthalates and liquid crystals,
dark clouds of dust and smoke, the roll of a thunderball
all home to gods and their demons. In the supernature
of unseen wires, unreal voices in the tongue of our creator,
in the holy flock of stern celestial eyes
and fires burning lightning quick in our great dark seas.
In the bromine and polymers, mercury and lead
of devices we must inter with respect when dead
lest the ether off carcasses left to rust
come back like unfinished souls to haunt us.

JOHN A. NIEVES

Tremble Island

I know the power of the dead is
not to talk but listen. The tides

are not angry, just violent.
This is less island than pressure
gauge needle. It doesn't know

you need it to survive
the speed of the stream. It doesn't
mean to throw you headlong

against all those red shells. If it did
send you down, it could not even
hear you drown. The dead are good

listeners. This island is not
the dead. If you have something
to say, nail it to a tree.

JOHN LOUGHLIN

Under the River Go the Faces of Everyone I Have Ever Loved

I think the world broke a world record today
For the number of people in it who cried.
Iggy Pop cried, as did most of Greenland.
Five hundred babies cried at exactly 2:43 AM
And another five hundred at 2:44. The President
Has a secret room where he likes to go shed tears.
Not even the Secret Service know about it.
What if I told you the President called me up
Crying? He did. I told him, *Buck up, little tomato.*
Talent scouts cried at the dearth of talent.
Frogs got the blues bad in the chemical bog.
Worst of all were the spilled milk drinkers
Who sobbed like it was the end of the world. It was.
When the devil cries, he sheds tears of real diamonds.
The contestant eliminated for making
A bland risotto cried, but thanked everyone
For the opportunity to cry. I got a surprise call
From my ex, who never calls, calling me in tears,
Something about her new husband's prognosis.
You could hear him in the background, banging
Around, lumbering, swearing to anyone how he
Was going to the kitchen to make some goddman eggs.
That's their secret passcode for *baby, let's fuck.*
You cried that time your pearl of toothpaste fell
Off its toothbrush and landed in the pedestal sink,
And you cried that time your car hit a mama deer
And it's gotten to the point like you and me and everyone
I know and even half-know, have been crying ever since.

The News

The dead knock at the door.
They arrive with big news.
The future as they imagined it,
The being dead part, hasn't turned out
As they expected. Both the idealists
And the realists had it wrong.
You will too, they tell you.
They tell you this as though
You're being handed a 1099 form
From the mostly pleasant librarian
Or a speeding ticket when you were
Only going five miles over the limit.
And with that, the dead turn around
And depart. Again. They walk out and
Enter the rain, which is how the dead
Get around. The dead's car.

Bios

KAVEH AKBAR founded and edits *Divedapper*. His poems appear in *American Poetry Review, Guernica, Poetry, Tin House*, and elsewhere. His debut full-length collection, *Calling a Wolf a Wolf*, will be published by Alice James Books in early 2018, and his chapbook, *Portrait of the Alcoholic* (2017), is available from Sibling Rivalry Press. Akbar was born in Tehran, Iran, and currently lives in Tallahassee.

Work by **JOSEPH AGUILAR** has appeared in *The Iowa Review, Okey-Panky, Tin House*, and *The Threepenny Review*. He is the author of the poetry collection, *Half Out Where* (Caketrain, 2014). He teaches at the University of Missouri and is currently working on a collaborative novel about hyper-intelligent dogs.

BRADLEY BAZZLE is a writer in Athens, Georgia. His stories have appeared in *Epoch, New England Review,* and *New Ohio Review,* and have won awards from *The Iowa Review* and *Third Coast.* He teaches writing at the University of Georgia and does improvisational comedy with Improv Athens.

AIMÉE BAKER's work has appeared in *Guernica, Massachusetts Review,* and *Southern Review.* The essay included in this issue of *Copper Nickel* is part of a larger series that focuses on the landscapes and experiences of living in rural upstate New York.

DAN BEACHY-QUICK is a poet, essayist, and occasional novelist, whose recent books include *gentlessness (*Tupelo Press, 2015) and *Shields & Shards & Stitches & Songs* (Omnidawn, 2015). His work has been supported by the Guggenheim and Lannan Foundations, and he teaches in the MFA program at Colorado State University.

ZEINA HASHEM BECK is a Lebanese poet. Her first book, *To Live in Autumn* (Backwaters Press, 2014), won the 2013 Backwaters Prize. Her second book, *Louder than Hearts* (Bauhan Publishing), won the 2016 May Sarton New Hampshire Poetry Prize and is forthcoming from Bauhan Publishing in April 2017.

ELEANOR MARY BOUDREAU has previously been published in *DIAGRAM* and *Denver Quarterly.* She lives in Tallahassee, Florida.

Originally from Lansing, Michigan, **JACOB BOYD** is currently pursuing a PhD at the University of Illinois at Chicago. Recent work can be found in *Blackbird, Midwest Review,* and *Notre Dame Review.*

ALLISON CAMPBELL is the author of the poetry collection *Encyclopédie of the Common & Encompassing* (Kore Press, 2016). She lives in New Orleans and teaches creative writing at Lusher Charter School. Her work has appeared in *The Cincinnati Review, Court Green, Rattle, Witness,* and elsewhere.

LUANNE CASTLE has published poetry and prose in *Grist, the museum of americana, Phoebe, River Teeth,* and elsewhere. Her first poetry collection, *Doll God* (Aldrich Press, 2015), won the New Mexico-Arizona Book Award. She divides her time between California and Arizona, where she shares land with a herd of javelina.

Work by **ALEX CHERTOK** appears or is forthcoming in *The Cincinnati Review, Literary Imagination, The Missouri Review, Quarterly West, Willow Springs, Best New Poets 2016,* and elsewhere. He received a fellowship from Virginia Center for the Creative Arts and currently teaches at Ithaca College and through the Cornell Prison Education Program.

KEVIN CRAFT is the editor of *Poetry Northwest.* His books include *Solar Prominence* (Cloudbank Books, 2005) and five volumes of the anthology *Mare Nostrum,* an annual collection of Italian translation and Mediterranean-inspired writing (Writ in Water Press, 2004-2009). His poems, essays, and reviews have appeared in *AGNI, Poetry, Ninth Letter,* and *Verse.*

STEPHANIE DICKINSON's work appears in *Bitter Oleander, Hotel Amerika, Los Angeles Review, Mudfish,* and elsewhere. Her seventh book—a novel—is *Love Highway* (Spuyten Duyvil, 2015). Previous books include the essay *Interview with Jean Seberg* (New Michigan Press, 2013) and a collection of prose poems, *Lust Series* (Spuyten Duyvil, 2011).

JOANNE DOMINIQUE DWYER has published in various journals, including *American Poetry Review, Gulf Coast, Poetry,* and *TriQuarterly.* Her first book of poems is *Bella Laide* (Sarabande, 2013).

DENISE EMMER is a Brazilian poet and cellist. For more information see page 91.

CODY ERNST's poetry appears in *Best New Poets, Bat City Review, The Minnesota Review,* and elsewhere. He is an instructor at The Writing Seminars at Johns Hopkins University and serves as a poetry editor of *The Adroit Journal.*

Poet, playwright, and novelist **ED FALCO** teaches at Virginia Tech. His poetry collection *Wolf Moon Blood Moon* is forthcoming from LSU in 2017, and his most recent novel is *Toughs* (Unbridled Books, 2014). He is the recipient of an NEA Fellowship, a Robert Penn Warren Prize from *The Southern Review*, and the Emily Clark Balch Prize from *Virginia Quarterly Review*. His work appears in *The Atlantic Monthly*, *The Best American Short Stories*, *Playboy*, and the *Pushcart Prize: Best of the Small Presses*.

ROBERT LONG FOREMAN's essays and short stories have won a Pushcart Prize and contests at *American Literary Review*, *The Cincinnati Review*, *The Journal*, and *Willow Springs*. Five of his essays have been listed as "Notable" in the *Best American Essays* anthologies. He lives in Kansas City.

KERRI FRENCH has published poetry in *Best New Poets*, *Barrow Street*, *The Journal*, *Mid-American Review*, and elsewhere. Dancing Girl Press published her chapbook of poems, *Instruments of Summer* (2013). She lives in Nashville, TN.

ANDREW GRACE's manuscript-in-progress is titled *The Last Will and Testament of Said Gun*. Sections have appeared recently or are forthcoming in *Alaska Quarterly Review*, *Columbia Poetry Review*, *Gettysburg Review*, and *Poetry Northwest*. He teaches at Kenyon College.

ALEXANDRA HAINES-STILES is a graduate of Harvard and Oxford, where she studied twentieth-century literature and language, as well as creative writing. Her work has appeared or is forthcoming in *Hanging Loose*, *Mays Anthology*, and elsewhere. She lives in New York and London.

RUTH JOFFRE's fiction, book reviews, and poetry can be found in *Kenyon Review*, *Hayden's Ferry Review*, *Prairie Schooner*, and elsewhere. She lives in Seattle, where she teaches creative writing at the Hugo House.

TIM KAHL is the author of *The String of Islands* (Dink, 2015) and *The Century of Travel* (CW Books, 2012). His work has been published in *Drunken Boat*, *Indiana Review*, *Mad Hatters' Review*, and *Prairie Schooner*. He is the editor of *Bald Trickster Press* and *Clade Song*, and vice president and events coordinator at The Sacramento Poetry Center. He teaches at California State University, Sacramento.

J. KATES is a poet and translator living in New Hampshire. Co-Director of Zephyr Press and former president of the American Literary Translators Association, he has received three NEA Fellowships and the Cliff Becker Prize in Translation, among other awards.

Originally from Philadelphia, **ASHLEY KEYSER** has lived in Chicago and the Ukraine. Her work has appeared in *Best New Poets 2015, The Cincinnati Review, The Journal,* and *Pleiades,* among others.

DANIELLE LAZARIN's debut collection, *Back Talk,* is forthcoming from Penguin Books in 2018. Her fiction has appeared in *Boston Review, Colorado Review, Indiana Review, Glimmer Train,* and elsewhere. She lives in her native New York, where she is at work on a novel.

DAVID DODD LEE is the author of ten books of poems, including *Animalities* (Four Way Books, 2014) and *Sky Booths in the Breath Somewhere* (BlazeVOX, 2010), a book of Ashberry erasure poems. He is also a visual artist. His artwork can be viewed at seventeenfingeredpoetrybird.blogspot.com.

ED BOK LEE is the author of *Whorled* (Coffee House Press, 2011), winner of a 2012 American Book Award and a 2012 Minnesota Book Award, and *Real Karaoke People* (New Rivers Press, 2005), winner of a 2006 PEN/Open Book Award and a 2006 Asian American Literary Award. His work has appeared or is forthcoming in *Idaho Review, Gulf Coast, Missouri Review,* and *Witness.* His forthcoming poetry collection will be published in 2018.

TOM LEGENDRE's previous work includes *The Burning* (Abacus, 2007) and *Half Life,* a play performed as part of NVA's art installation of the same name in conjunction with The National Theatre of Scotland. He is a Lecturer in Creative Writing at the University of Nottingham.

ESTHER LIN's poems appear in *Adroit, Crazyhorse, Guernica, Vinyl,* and elsewhere. She has received fellowships from Poets House and the Queens Council on the Arts and currently teaches at Queens College, CUNY.

JOHN LOUGHLIN's poems have appeared in a variety of journals, including *Black Warrior Review, Colorado Review, Drunken Boat,* and *Ploughshares.* He works as a Sales Manager in Chicago's Loop.

JAMES DAVIS MAY's first book of poetry, *Unquiet Things,* was published by Louisiana State University Press in March of 2016.

JOHN McCARTHY's work has appeared in *Best New Poets 2015, The Jabberwock Review, The Minnesota Review,* and *Salamander.* He is the 2016 winner of the Pinch Literary Award in Poetry. He is the author of *Ghost Country* (Midwestern Gothic Press, 2016).

JENNY MOLBERG's debut collection, *Marvels of the Invisible*, won the 2014 Berkshire Prize and is forthcoming from Tupelo Press. Her poems appear in *Best New Poets*, *The Adroit Journal*, *The Missouri Review*, *Poetry International*, and elsewhere. She lives in Warrensburg, MO, where she teaches at the University of Central Missouri and coedits *Pleiades*.

PATRICIA MURPHY's work has appeared in *American Poetry Review*, *The Iowa Review*, *The Massachusetts Review*, and *New Orleans Review*.

JOHN A. NIEVES has poems forthcoming or recently published in *Cincinnati Review*, *Crazyhorse*, *Pleiades*, *The Literary Review*, and elsewhere. He won the *Indiana Review* Poetry Contest and his first book, *Curio* (Elixir, 2014), won the Elixir Press Annual Poetry Award Judge's Prize. He teaches at Salisbury University.

WENDY OLESON's recent prose and poetry appear in *Hotel Amerika, Memorious,* and *Quarterly West*. She won the 2015 *storySouth* Million Writers Award and teachings for the Writers' Program at UCLA Extension.

PEDRO PONCE is the author of *Stories After Goya* (Tree Light Books,2014) and *Alien Autopsy* (Cow Heavy Books, 2010). His fiction has appeared in *Alaska Quarterly Review*, *Gigantic*, *PANK*, *Ploughshares*, and other journals. A 2012 National Endowment for the Arts fellow in creative writing, he teaches at St. Lawrence University.

TODD PORTNOWITZ is a recipient of the 2015 Raiziss/de Palchi Fellowship from the Academy of American Poets. His work has appeared in *Poetry, Modern Poetry in Translation, The Cortland Review* and *PN Review*.

LORENZO CARLUCCI is an Italian poet and a professor of mathematical logic at the University of Rome "La Sapienza." For more information, see page 13.

ALICITA RODRÍGUEZ is a Cuban-American writer living in Denver. Her work appears in *New Flash Fiction Review*, *Wreckage of Reason II,* and *Your Impossible Voice*. She is currently working on a creative nonfiction book about Operation Pedro Pan, the exodus of more than 14,000 unaccompanied children from Cuba to the US in the early 1960s.

J. ALLYN ROSSER's fourth collection of poems, *Mimi's Trapeze* (2014), was published by the University of Pittsburgh Press. Her work has been awarded the Morse Prize, the New Criterion Poetry Prize, and *Poetry* magazine's Bock and Wood prizes. She has received fellowships from the Lannan and Guggenheim Foundations, and the National Endowment for the Arts. She teaches at Ohio University, where she has served as Editor-in-Chief of *New Ohio Review* for the past eight years.

THADDEUS RUTKOWSKI's work has appeared in *Pleiades, Potomac Review, The New York Times*, and others. His book *Violent Outbursts* was published in January 2016 by Spuyten Duyvil Press, and he was awarded a fellowship from the New York Foundation for the Arts. He currently teaches at Medgar Evers College.

ERIN KATE RYAN's fiction has appeared in *Glimmer Train, Conjunctions, A cappella Zoo*, and *Hayden's Ferry Review*. She's been awarded fellowships and grants from the Millay Colony, the Edward Albee Foundation, and the Hambidge Center for Creative Arts & Sciences. She is the recipient of a Bread Loaf Writers' Conference scholarship, and a 2016 Minnesota Artist's Initiative grant.

MATTHEW SALESSES is the author of the novel *The Hundred-Year Flood* (Little A/ Amazon books), and the forthcoming *The Murder of the Doppelganger* (2018), and the collection of essays *Own Story* (2019). Matthew has received awards and fellowships from the Bread Loaf Writers' Conference, *Glimmer Train, Mid-American Review, [PANK], HTMLGIANT*, Inprint, and elsewhere.

RYAN SHARP's poetry and reviews appear in several journals, including *Berkeley Poetry Review, Callaloo, DIALOGIST, [PANK]*, and elsewhere. He lives in Austin, Texas, edits *Borderlands: Texas Poetry Review*, and serves as the Writers' Studio Coordinator at Huston-Tillotson University.

TATIANA SHCHERBINA is a Russian poet living in Moscow. For more information, see page 155.

S. FARRELL SMITH's work has appeared recently in *Ascent, Hippocampus Magazine*, and the anthology *Oh, Baby!* from *Creative Nonfiction*. Her essays have been listed as "Special Mention" in *Pushcart Prize: Best of the Small Presses* and "Notable" in *Best American Essays*. She lives in Connecticut.

T. D. STORM is the winner of Salem College's Reynolds Price Short Fiction Award. His fiction has been published by *Black Warrior Review, Boston Literary Magazine, Short Story America* and others.

YERRA SUGARMAN is the author of two poetry collections: *Forms of Gone* and *The Bag of Broken Glass*, both from Sheep Meadow Press. She has received a 2011 NEA Fellowship and awards from PEN American Center, the Canada Council for the Arts, the Poetry Society of America, and *The Nation* magazine.

ADAM TAVEL is the author of *The Fawn Abyss* (Salmon Poetry, 2016), and *Plash & Levitation* (University of Alaska Press, 2015), winner of the Permafrost Book Prize.

PIMONE TRIPLETT is the author of *Rumor* (Triquarterly, 2009), *The Price of Light* (Four Way Books, 2005) and *Ruining the Picture* (Triquarterly/Northwestern, 1998). She teaches at the University of Washington and in the Warren Wilson MFA Program for Writers. She is the co-editor of *Poet's Work, Poet's Play* (University of Michigan Press, 2007), a collection of essays on craft.

SASHA WEST's poems have appeared in *Ninth Letter, Forklift, Ohio, Third Coast, The Journal, Canary*, and elsewhere. Her first book of poems, *Failure and I Bury the Body* (Harper Perennial, 2013), won the National Poetry Series and the Texas Institute of Letters Bob Bush First Book of Poetry Award.

CANDACE WILLIAMS is "a black queer nerd" who has won a Brooklyn Poets Fellowship and directs community operations for a startup. Her work appears in *Bennington Review, Lambda Literary Review*, and *Sixth Finch*.

Required Reading

(issue 24)

(Each issue we ask our contributors to recommend three or so recent titles. What follows is the list generated by this issue's contributors.)

César Aira, *An Episode in the Life of a Landscape Painter*, trans. Chris Andrews (Todd Portnowitz)

Mia Alvar, *In the Country: Stories* (Patricia Colleen Murphy)

Carlos Drummond de Andrade, *Multitudinous Heart: Selected Poems*, trans. Richard Zenith (Tim Kahl)

Branka Arsic, *Bird Relics: Grief and Vitalism in Thoreau* (Dan Beachy-Quick)

A. Igoni Barrett, *Blackass* (Pedro Ponce)

Joshua Bennett, *The Sobbing School* (Jenny Molberg)

Justin Boening, *Not on the Last Day, But on the Very Last* (Sasha West)

Bruce Bond, *Black Anthem* (Adam Tavel)

Shane Book, *Congotronic* (Pimone Triplett)

Marci Calabretta Cancio-Bello, *Hour of the Ox* (Luanne Castle)

Laurie Jean Cannady, *Crave: Sojourn of a Hungry Soul* (S. Farrell Smith)

Eds. Max King Cap, Beth Loffreda, & Claudia Rankine, *The Racial Imaginary: Writers on Race and the Life of the Mind* (Pimone Triplett)

Jos Charles, *Safe Space* (Kaveh Akbar)

Katie Chase, *Man and Wife* (Sasha West)

Jennifer S. Cheng, *House A* (Sasha West)

Franny Choi, *Floating, Brilliant, Gone* (Erin Kate Ryan)

Jace Clayton, *Uproot: Travels in 21ˢᵗ-Century Music and Digital Culture* (Andrew Grace)

Ta-Nehisi Coates, *Between the World and Me* (Jenny Molberg)

Jonathan Culler, *Theory of the Lyric* (Jacob Boyd)

Katie Egan Cunningham, *Story: Still the Heart of Literacy Learning* (S. Farrell Smith)

Charles D'Ambrosio, *Loitering* (David Dodd Lee)

Kamel Daoud, *Meursault, contre-enquête* (J. Kates)

Marcy Dermansky, *The Red Car* (Matthew Salesses)

Matthew Desmond, *Evicted: Poverty and Profit in the American City* (Ruth Joffre)

Colin Dickey, *Ghostland* (Erin Kate Ryan)

Dolores Dorantes, *Style*, trans. Jen Hofer (Matthew Salesses)

Jehanne Dubrow, *The Arranged Marriage* (Yerra Sugarman)

Patricia Duncker, *Sophie and the Sibyl* (Thomas Legendre)

Steven Dunn, *Potted Meat* (Joseph Aguilar)

Mohsen Emadi, *Standing on Earth*, trans. Lyn Coffin (Kaveh Akbar)

Pamela Erens, *Eleven Hours* (Danielle Lazarin)

Martin Espada, *Vivas to Those Who Failed* (Zeina Hashem Beck)

Brian Evenson, *A Collapse of Horses* (Bradley Bazzle)

Brian Evenson, *The Warren* (Robert Long Foreman)

Gemma Files, *Experimental Film* (Wendy Oleson)

Matthew Gavin Frank, *The Mad Feast* (Aimée Baker)

Rebecca Morgan Frank, *The Spokes of Venus* (Allison Campbell)

Thomas Frank, *Listen Liberal: Or, What Ever Happened to the Party of the People?* (Robert Long Foreman)

Abby Frucht & Laurie Alberts, *A Well-Made Bed* (S. Farrell Smith)

Alice Fulton, *Barely Composed* (Alex Chertok)

Joanna Fuhrman, *The Year of Yellow Butterflies* (Yerra Sugarman)

Nicola Gardini, *Lost Words*, trans. Michael F. Moore (Stephanie Dickinson)

Ross Gay, *catalog of unabashed gratitude* (Zeina Hashem Beck)

Stephen Gibson, *Self-Portrait in a Door-Length Mirror* (Ed Falco)

Alan Gillis, *Scapegoat* (Thomas Legendre)

Aracelis Girmay, *The Black Maria* (Adam Tavel)

Jennifer Givhan, *Landscape with Headless Mama* (Kerri French)

Elizabeth T. Gray, Jr, *Series / India* (Joanne Dominique Dwyer)

Kimberly Grey, *The Opposite of Light* (John McCarthy)

Becky Hagenston, *Scavengers: Collected Stories* (Wendy Oleson)

Yuval Noah Harari, *Sapiens: A Brief History of Humankind* (J. Allyn Rosser)

Joy Harjo, *Conflict Resolution for Holy Beings* (Ed Bok Lee)

francine j. harris, *play dead* (Kaveh Akbar)

Kathryn Harrison, *True Crimes: A Family Album* (Thaddeus Rutkowski)

Elsa Hart, *The White Mirror* (Thaddeus Rutkowski)

Matt Hart, *Radiant Action* (Cody Ernst)

Terrance Hayes, *How to Be Drawn* (Jacob Boyd, Ryan Sharp)

Virginia Heffernan, *Magic and Loss: The Internet as Art* (Alexandra Haines-Stiles)

Sarah Helm, *Ravensbruck* (Stephanie Dickinson)

David Hernandez, *Dear, Sincerely* (Allison Campbell)

Tony Hoagland, *Application for Release from the Dream* (Joanne Dominique Dwyer, Yerra Sugarman)

Ishion Hutchinson, *House of Lords and Commons* (Todd Portnowitz)

Hope Jahren, *Lab Girl* (Patricia Colleen Murphy)

Tyehimba Jess, *Olio* (Ryan Sharp)

Adam Johnson, *Fortune Smiles* (T. D. Storm)

Troy Jollimore, *Syllabus of Errors* (Kevin Craft)

W. Todd Kaneko, *The Dead Wrestler Elegies* (Aimée Baker)

Han Kang, *The Vegetarian* (Matthew Salesses)

Robin Kimmerer, *Braiding Sweetgrass* (Ed Bok Lee)

Kim Krans, *ABC Dream* (Alicita Rodríguez)

Bridget Lee, *Sun Creatures* (Ed Bok Lee)

Ursula K. Le Guin, *The Found and the Lost: The Collected Novellas of Ursula K. Le Guin* (David Dodd Lee)

Jill Leovy, *Ghettoside* (Bradley Bazzle)

Ben Lerner, *The Hatred of Poetry* (Eleanor Mary Boudreau)

Ben Lerner, *10:04* (Ed Falco)

Dana Levin, *Banana Palace* (Eleanor Mary Boudreau)

Larry Levis, *The Darkening Trapeze* (Jacob Boyd)

Robin Coste Lewis, *Voyage of the Sable Venus* (Ryan Sharp)

Ada Limón, *Bright Dead Things* (Zeina Hashem Beck, Kevin Craft, Danielle Lazarin, James Davis May)

Grevel Lindop, *Luna Park* (Adam Tavel)

Kelly Link, *Get in Trouble* (Ruth Joffre, T. D. Storm)

Clarice Lispector, *Collected Stories* (Ashley Keyser)

Karan Mahajan, *The Association of Small Bombs* (Todd Portnowitz)

Salgado Maranhão, *Tiger Fur*, trans. Alexis Levitin (Tim Kahl)

Nate Marshall, *Wild Hundreds* (Andrew Grace)

Amelia Martens, *The Spoons in the Grass Are There to Dig a Moat* (Robert Long Foreman)

Ian McEwan, *Nutshell* (Alexandra Haines-Stiles)

Susana Medina, *Philosophical Toys* (Pedro Ponce)

Wayne Miller, *Post-* (Eleanor Mary Boudreau)

Patricia Colleen Murphy, *Hemming Flames* (Thomas Legendre)

Raduan Nasser, *Ancient Tillage*, trans. Karen Sherwood Sotelino (Stephanie Dickinson)

Amy Newman, *On This Day in Poetry History* (John A. Nieves)

Celeste Ng, *Everything I Never Told You* (James Davis May)

Kathryn Nuernberger, *The End of Pink* (Jenny Molberg, John A. Nieves)

Christina Olivares, *No Map of the Earth Includes Stars* (Danielle Lazarin)

Azareen Van der Vliet Oloomi, *Fra Keeler* (Joseph Aguilar)

Cynthia Ozick, *Critics, Monsters, Fanatics, and Other Literary Essays* (Ashley Keyser)

Pat Parker, *The Complete Works of Pat Parker* (Candace Williams)

Charlotte Pence, *Many Small Fires* (James Davis May)

Emilia Phillips, *Groundspeed* (Aimée Baker)

Catherine Pierce, *The Tornado Is the World* (Allison Campbell)

Alejandra Pizarnik, *Extracting the Stone of Madness: Poems 1962-1972*, trans. Yvette Siegert (Joseph Aguilar)

Stanley Plumly, *Against Sunset* (Kevin Craft)

Naomi Pomeroy, *Taste and Technique* (John Loughlin)

Max Porter, *Grief Is the Thing with Feathers* (Alexandra Haines-Stiles)

Courtney Queeney, *Filibuster to Delay a Kiss* (John McCarthy)

Sam Quinones, *Dreamland: The True Tale of America's Opiate Epidemic* (Andrew Grace)

Lawrence Raab, *Mistaking Each Other for Ghosts* (J. Allyn Rosser)

Stephanie Rogers, *Plucking the Stinger* (Kerri French)

Martha Ronk, *Transfer of Qualities* (Dan Beachy-Quick)

Tomasz Różycki, *Colonies*, trans. Mira Rosenthal (Tim Kahl)

Tomasz Różycki, *Twelve Stations*, trans. Bill Johnston (J. Kates)

Selah Saterstrom, *Slab* (Pedro Ponce)

Nicole Sealey, *The Animal After Whom Other Animals Are Named* (Esther Lin)

Frederick Seidel, *Widening Income Inequality* (Cody Ernst)

Diane Seuss, *Four-Legged Girl* (Joanne Dominique Dwyer, Esther Lin)

Jon Silkin, *Complete Poems* (J. Kates)

Austin Smith, *Almanac* (John McCarthy)

Nick Srnicek & Alex Williams, *Inventing the Future* (Candace Williams)

Gloria Steinem, *My Life on the Road* (Patricia Colleen Murphy)

Sarah Sweeney, *Tell Me If You're Lying* (Kerri French)

John Tipton, *Paramnesia* (Dan Beachy-Quick)

Leo Tolstoy, *Anna Karenina*, trans. Rosamund Bartlett (a new translation) (J. Allyn Rosser)

Justin Torres, *We the Animals* (Ed Falco)

Frank Viva, *Outstanding in the Rain* (Alicita Rodríguez)

Arthur Vogelsang, *Orbit* (David Dodd Lee)

Ocean Vuong, *Night Sky with Exit Wounds* (Ruth Joffre)

Colson Whitehead, *The Underground Railroad* (Thaddeus Rutkowski)

Joy Williams, *Ninety-Nine Stories of God* (Cody Ernst)

Joy Williams, *The Visiting Privilege: New and Collected Stories* (Wendy Oleson)

Jane Wong, *Overpour* (Pimone Triplett)

C. D. Wright, *The Poet, the Lion, Talking Pictures, El Farolito, a Wedding in St. Roch, the Big Box Store, the Warp in the Mirror, Spring, Midnight, Fire & All* (Eleanor Mary Boudreau)

Wendy Xu, *Naturalism* (Candace Williams)

The Copper Nickel Editors' Prizes

(est. 2015)

(Two $500 prizes awarded to the most exciting work published in each issue, as determined by a vote of the Copper Nickel staff)

Past Winners

fall 2016 (issue 23)

Tim Carter, poetry

Evelyn Somers, prose

spring 2016 (issue 22)

Bernard Farai Matambo, poetry

Sequoia Nagamatsu, prose

fall 2015 (issue 21)

Jonathan Weinert, poetry

Tyler Mills, prose

spring 2015 (issue 20)

Michelle Oakes, poetry

Donovan Ortega, prose

COPPER NICKEL & MILKWEED EDITIONS
present

THE JAKE ADAM YORK PRIZE

for a first or second poetry collection

($2,000 + a standard royalty contract
+ publication by Milkweed Editions)

submission deadline:
October 15, 2017

final judge: **TBA**

for more info:
copper-nickel.org/bookprize/

FORTHCOMING SPRING 2017

the *Southern* *Review*

POETRY

Lindsey D. Alexander, Bruce Beasley, Bruce Cohen, Brendan Galvin,
Stephen Gibson, Leah Naomi Green, Jeff Hardin, Jeff Hoffman,
Patricia Hooper, Paul Hunter, Mark Irwin, Michael McFee, Steve Myers,
Ricardo Pau-Llosa, David Petruzelli, Catherine Pierce, Kevin Prufer,
Charles Rafferty, Elizabeth Rees, Cathie Sandstrom, Carrie Shipers, R. T. Smith,
Joannie Stangeland, Chelsea Wagenaar, Brian Phillip Whalen, Michele Wolf

FICTION

Marjorie Celona, Robert Hahn, Nicholas Mainieri, Iheoma Nwachukwu,
Amy Silverberg

NONFICTION

Sandra Gail Lambert, Paul Lindholdt

VISUAL ART

paintings by Ramiro Gomez

milkweed
editions

CHRIS SANTIAGO
Tula
WINNER OF THE 2016 LINDQUIST & VENNUM PRIZE FOR POETRY

———

ROSA ALICE BRANCO
Cattle of the Lord
TRANSLATED FROM THE PORTUGUESE BY ALEXIS LEVITIN

———

CHRISTOPHER HOWELL
Love's Last Number

———

KATHY FAGAN
Sycamore

———

REBECCA DUNAHM
Cold Pastoral

———

WILLIAM BREWER
I Know Your Kind
WINNER OF THE 2016 NATIONAL POETRY SERIES

MILKWEED.ORG

COPPERNICKEL

subscription rates

For regular folks:

one year (two issues)—$20
two years (four issues)—$35
three years (six issues)—$45
five years (ten issues)—$60

For student folks:

one year (two issues)—$15
two years (four issues)—$23
three years (six issues)—$32
five years (ten issues)—$50

For more information, visit: www.copper-nickel.org.

To go directly to subscriptions
visit: www.regonline.com/coppernickelsubscriptions.

To order back issues, call 303-556-4026
or email wayne.miller@ucdenver.edu.